Jews for Jesus

Jews for Jesus

Moishe Rosen
with
William Proctor

FLEMING H. REVELL COMPANY
Old Tappan, New Jersey

Unless otherwise indicated, all Scripture quotations in this volume are from the King James Version of the Bible.

The Scripture quotation identified as RSV is from the Revised Standard Version of the Bible, Copyrighted 1946 and 1952, and used by permission.

The selection "Passover Lamb" is by Sam Nadler, copyright © 1973 by Sam Nadler.

The selection "Praise Him, Praise Him" is from "Music for the Messiah—Songs of Jews for Jesus," copyright © 1972 by Stuart Dauermann.

Library of Congress Cataloging in Publication Data

Rosen, Moishe.
    Jews for Jesus

    1. Missions to Jews. 2. Rosen, Moishe.
3. Converts from Judaism. I. Proctor, William,
joint author. II. Title.
BV2623.R58A34   248'.246   73-22169
ISBN 0-8007-0638-2

CONTENTS

PREFACE

Because my life has involved more action than contemplation, it's natural that this story, which is largely a personal account, should focus on encounter and confrontation, rather than on doctrine and theory. The events and anecdotes, some of which are composite accounts, actually occurred, though on occasion the identities of individuals have been changed.

When a Jew claims to believe in Jesus, he is sure to generate controversy. I can only hope that the controversial passages in this book will not obscure the overriding purpose, which is to convey the tremendous impact that the Messiah has had on me and on the other Jews for Jesus.

MOISHE ROSEN

Jews for Jesus

1 WHAT'S A NICE JEWISH BOY
   LIKE YOU . . . ?

Multicolored neon lights flashed their messages of seduction up and down the three-block strip of Broadway in San Francisco's North Beach section. On one corner over Big Al's place stood a sign depicting a twenties-type gangland figure with machine gun in hand; across the street at The Garden of Eden the voluptuous figure of a naked Eve lounged near a thirty-foot palm tree entwined by a leering serpent. Flashily-dressed, hard-eyed barkers stood in doorways, shouting and vying for the patronage of the tourists. The streets were crowded with baby-faced sailors in their spotless whites, sequin-sweatered matrons arm in arm with their balding husbands, hip-looking kids in old casual clothes, and visiting kids just trying to look hip for the weekend.

"Naked, naked, naked!" shouted the barkers at passersby.

"The hottest sex show in town! No cover, and no cover charge!"

One of the barkers smiled humorlessly as his steely eyes sized up a hesitant young sailor. He leaned forward, grabbed the serviceman by the arm, and whispered, "Hey, man, just take a peek. It won't cost you anything," and the boy in white was propelled through the curtained door. The rest of the crowd, some looking sheepish, some bewildered, others boisterously high-spirited, milled on past to gawk at other doorways plastered with photographs of nudes. The marquees boasted: CO-EDS IN THE NUDE, THIS PLACE HAS BEEN RAIDED BY THE POLICE 24 TIMES, and ON STAGE—LIVE SEX ACT!

The setting was just right for us to launch our counteroffensive. Wearing denim jackets embroidered with "Jesus Made Me Kosher," and "Jews for Jesus," about twenty of us formed a picket line. We marched around in a tight oval, holding up placards which proclaimed slogans such as GOD'S LOVE LASTS; LOVE, NOT LUST; and JESUS IS COMING AGAIN. Our objective: to get the potential customers to think about where they were and what they were about to do. We knew if they took a good look at themselves, they might go home rather than waste their money and minds on a cheap sex show.

The nudie go-go bars had never exactly received us with open arms because we drove away their business. The atmosphere seemed especially hostile that night, but we were as loud as ever as we started our first chant: "Love, not lust! Love, not lust!" That's when the trouble began.

A Jewish woman, who had been whispering to one of the barkers, broke away from the crowd that had gathered to watch us and screamed, "That's my religion you're ridiculing!" Shouting a stream of obscenities, she began tearing up our placards and kicking several of the girls in our group. Finally, she pulled out a pair of scissors and started stabbing at some of the marchers.

At first, I thought she would get tired and leave when we didn't respond to her attacks. Our commitment to nonviolence has taught us that refusing to react can often prevent the escalation of violence. But that tactic was not working with this half-crazed woman, so I sent Bruce Skoropinski, one of our group leaders, to get the police. I then grabbed a placard, which proclaimed: GOD LOVES YOU!, away from a girl who was under attack and managed to get the woman to shift her rage toward me. The ploy worked all too well. She stabbed me again and again in the arm with her scissors and finally succeeded in inflicting a deep wound on my hand.

As the blood rushed down my arm and onto the sidewalk, bystanders began to scream and call for help. I was frightened, too, but I had enough wits about me to yell, "They're attacking me because I'm a Jew for Jesus! This bar condones violence because they don't like Jesus!"

As is our custom, none of the other marchers came to my defense. They just kept marching because if they had stopped, the demonstration would probably have quickly dissolved. We could then have been arrested for loitering, under an ordinance that requires demonstrators to keep moving in an orderly line. And if owners of those bars knew they could break up our demonstrations by hurting us, they would continue to encourage the violence.

Marcia Goldstein, who participated in the protest, remembers some of the subsequent events better than I do: "Moishe was bleeding like crazy, but he kept picketing, trailing blood behind him on the sidewalk. He held his sign up high, and the blood was running down his arm onto his denim jacket. There was enough blood on the sidewalk for us to slide around on. The woman got more and more angry because he wouldn't give her his placard. I guess the star of David painted in the background on the sign was what annoyed her so much."

The reason I held my bloody arm up in the air was not to show off my wounds. I was trying to slow the bleeding and prevent myself from becoming too weak to appear on a radio program that was scheduled a half hour later. Some bystanders finally held the woman away from me, and I was able to get a towel from one of the nearby restaurants to use as a makeshift bandage. By the time the police arrived, I had managed to stop most of the bleeding.

Steffi Geiser, my main adviser, or *consigliere* as I like to call her, volunteered to accompany me to the radio studio. But before I left, I had one final request for those who stayed behind: "Do one thing for me. Demonstrate here an hour longer than you usually would, to show them that a little blood's not going to stop us."

As we drove to the radio studio, I fought the lightheadedness that was starting to creep over me from the loss of blood. And I prayed that God would give me the strength to get through the show. I must have looked strange, gesturing with my hand in a bloody towel, as I sat there between the moderator and another minister who was also on the program. But God answered my prayers. I didn't begin to feel really weak until the doctor at a nearby hospital sewed me up after the show was finished.

Steffi and I drove back through the North Beach section on our way home, just to make sure that the others had left safely. Sitting quietly in the car, I surveyed the tawdry signs and the lonely people who were peering through the open doors hoping to get a fleeting glance at the naked dancers. Then I looked down at myself: My bloody denim jacket had "Jews for Jesus" embroidered on the back, and there were campaign buttons all over my chest with slogans, "Jesus is a Jew," "Torah is Good for the Soul," and so on. Here I am, I thought, a middle-aged man who always had the reputation of being a sober, reserved, stable fellow. Although my mother had been dead for several years, I could almost hear her whispering in my ear, "Moishe, what's a nice Jewish boy like you doing in a place like this?"

2 THE JEWISH BIRTHRIGHT

Jews come in all shapes and sizes. Some are blonds, some brunettes, some fiery redheads. But although there is no single Jewish physical type, there is a distinctive Jewish identity. I can talk to a person for five minutes, and no matter what he looks like, I can usually tell whether or not he's Jewish by the way he responds to talk about Jesus.

What's the essence of the Jewish mystique? Part of it is a shared life experience, which begins in the earliest childhood years. We Jews have always stood apart from the surrounding community. For the male child this separation begins with an ancient and rather painful physical seal—the ceremony of circumcision on the eighth day after birth. Most male gentile children are circumcised for hygienic purposes, but there is a more profound meaning to the Jewish rite than good medicine. My birth certificate gives my name as Martin Meyer Rosen, but I was also given the Hebrew name Moishe, or Moses, at my circumcision. In the presence of the required *minyan,* or ten men, a *mohel* (a rabbi especially trained to do circumcision) performed the ceremony in Kansas City, Missouri, my birthplace. I thus entered into the *bris,* or covenant, which God commanded Abraham and his descendants to observe in Genesis 17:10.

Jewish tradition and culture run deep on both sides of my family. My mother's parents, Reform Jews from Austria, immigrated to this country through the port of Hamburg, Germany. My father's father, a well-to-do Russian factory owner who was an Orthodox believer, had to flee with his family to America because of persecutions against Jews in his homeland. My father and mother met and married in Kansas City in 1928, and I was born in 1932 during the depths of the depression. Unable to find work in Missouri, my dad moved to Denver when I was only two years old. After years of proud poverty and several jobs that never quite fed the family, my father found security, then prosperity, in the scrap-metal business.

My earliest recollection of being different from the other kids was when I was a first grader at a Denver elementary school. The Christmas holidays were approaching, and my teacher began to teach us Christmas carols. The first song I learned was "Silent Night," and I came home eager to show my mother how well I could sing it. But when I reached the "Round yon virgin, mother and child" lyrics, she interrupted the performance with a smile and a hand on my shoulder.

"You sing nice, Moishe, but that's not our kind of song," she said. "I want you to be sure you don't sing it around your grandfather, because it would upset him."

"Why? Is it like saying bad words, Mama?" I asked.

"That's a song for the Christians, not for the Jews. Jesus is the God for the Christians, but He isn't for us."

I wondered what a Christian was, but whatever it was I knew I wasn't one.

I continued to sing along with the kids at school, but I never sang any more Christmas carols around my family. I didn't even really mind that Santa Claus and the other trappings of Christmas were not recognized at my home, because we had a good substitute. We could always expect Judas Maccabaeus to bring presents during our December Chanukah celebration.

But my sense of separation as a Jew in Denver was not always so easy and peaceful. When I was about seven years old, I can remember my mother and father sitting with their ears glued to our radio, their faces tense and pale. They were listening to Adolf Hitler who, in a torrent of angry German, was denouncing the United States as a weak country run by the Jews. Both of my parents spoke fluent Yiddish, which resembles German. They could understand most of what Hitler was saying, and his words, a hemisphere away, frightened them.

Anti-Semitism became a personal issue in my own life shortly afterwards. Feeling adventurous, I decided to do some exploring outside my own lower-middle-class Jewish neighborhood. After a journey of about ten blocks, I noticed some boys playing in an empty lot. We struck up a conversation, and they seemed friendly enough.

"Where do you live?" asked one of the boys.

I told him, and he replied, "Oh, that's over in Jew town. Are you a Jew?"

I shrugged and said, "Yes."

The boy then jeered and spit at me, and the others began to toss clods of clay. That was the last time I tried any exploring outside my own neighborhood, and I also learned a very useful conversational tactic for a Jewish boy. If anyone asked me whether I was a Jew, I would answer, "Why do you want to know?"

Despite the rejections I sometimes experienced in the world at large, I always felt accepted and reasonably secure at home. The depression and an injury my father had suffered kept us rather poor during the early years of my life, but we had a sense of solidarity and pride as a family. My father was not very religious, but he and my mother insisted that my younger brother Don and I attend a local *cheder,* or Hebrew school. I learned some Hebrew, various prayers, and the meaning of different Jewish traditions and holidays. As I recall, there was no discussion of religious belief, and that was all right with me. Though my father attended synagogue, he often told us, "Religion is a racket." I developed a similar cynicism after my *Bar Mitzvah,* the Jewish confirmation at which a young man accepts responsibility for his own sin and becomes duty-bound to follow Jewish law.

Though my father was disenchanted with Jewish religious leadership, he expected the family to observe certain traditions. He always got off work on the *yom tov,* or holidays, such as *Yom Kippur* (the Day of Atonement) and *Rosh Hashana* (the Jewish New Year), and we went to my grandfather's house and to synagogue. I had to wear the *yarmulkah,* or skull cap, and a *tallis katan,* a garment with fringes (*tzizit*) required by Jewish law to be worn inside the shirt.

Through a shrewd business sense and hard work, my dad managed to open his own scrap-iron business, and he lost no time in instructing me about the secret of his success. He spent about an hour every evening teaching me and my brother Don his philosophy of life, which was a combination of the Jewish sense of culture and achievement and his own brand of homey diligence. Dad periodically made sure we could recite our Hebrew prayers, and he stressed business principles that would make a valuable course in any business school: how to deal with people, how to determine the value of an item, and how to buy and sell.

He also insisted that both his sons learn how to work, and so at nine years of age I became involved in part-time chores in the family business. I was taking apart automobile motors when I was twelve and using a twenty-pound sledgehammer on cast iron at thirteen. But after a couple of years working part-time after school and full time during the summers, I decided I wanted to keep my hands clean and save my back for other pursuits. That was a momentous decision for me, because it meant I had to cut a significant tie with the family and look for a job in the gentile world.

In my first foray into this strange *goyish* environment I applied for a part-time job as a clerk in a Denver manufacturing plant. There was no fair-employment legislation in those days, of course. The personnel director said, "Well, you're certainly qualified for this job, and I'd like to give you a shot at this, but we have a problem. Our com-

pany has never employed anyone of your race before, and I don't
think it would be wise for you to be the first."

I was disappointed, but I didn't push the point because I knew
there was no sense in it. I finally found a job with a Jewish firm, but
not before I had filed away an important lesson in my mind. My job-
hunting had confirmed what I had learned at home—that there were
two kinds of people in the world, *us* and *them*. *Them* included all
non-Jews, or Gentiles, or Christians. They were all the same in my
book. I thought that most people were Christians, and that most of
these Christians were against Jews. My identity as a Jew was a condition of birth, and I assumed that the same thing was true of Christians. Like many Jewish people, I was unable to distinguish between
a genuine Christian who has made a commitment to Christ and a
culturally-Christian Gentile.

This sense of separation and of rejection by the gentile majority
reached a climax when I joined a National Guard artillery unit at
the tender age of fifteen. I had lied about my age and managed to get
accepted because I looked older and had already grown to my full
height of six feet two. We were activated in the late 1940s because
of a crisis with the Soviet Union in Berlin, and I was quite excited
until I realized the kind of guy we had for a battery first sergeant. He
was a blatant, outspoken anti-Semite and frequently made obnoxious,
insulting remarks to me in the presence of the other enlisted men:
"Tell me, Rosen, are all Jewish women whores or just your mother?"

I knew he was trying to goad me into a fight. Many of the other
guys in my battery were acquaintances from my high school, but none
of them would come over and say, "Hey, Rosen, we don't feel that
way." It was me against the whole unit, or so I thought.

There was only one other Jew in our entire battalion, and I think
I disliked him even more than the sergeant because he seemed to
encourage people to insult him. Some of the guys would always say,
"Sheeny, sheeny," when they passed him, and he'd just grin at the
insult. One time a group stopped him and demanded, "Show us your
circumcision," and he dutifully complied while they snickered.

I went over to him after the others had left and kicked him in the
behind. "You want to make a fool out of yourself, then make a fool
out of yourself," I shouted. "But don't make a fool out of our people.
When they rag you for being a Jew, stand up to them!"

The fellows in my unit knew I wouldn't stand for any insults from
them. I had gotten into too many fights for being a Jew when I was
younger, as many of them were acutely aware. But that first sergeant

was another matter. He not only continued to make obscene remarks to me, but he also refused to give me my mail on time, thus forcing me to ask him for it. One day he said, "Rosen, have you been a good little Jew today? If you've been a good Jew and said all your sheeny prayers, maybe I'll give you this letter."

"The law says you have to give it to me," I replied.

"So what are you going to do, Rosen? Go to the inspector general?"

"I just might," I replied, but in those days the inspector general might not be available for weeks at a time.

These pressures finally got to me. One day, I was by myself in the barracks when the sergeant came in and made some obnoxious remark. As he was bending over inspecting someone's locker, I picked up a carbine and hit him with the butt across the side of his head. It felt so good to hurt him that I became a little frightened by my own anger and potential for violence.

"You'll kill me," he cried, as I stood over him with the weapon.

"Good," I said. "That's great. It's what you need." Everything I hated about *them*—Christians, the entire non-Jewish world—had culminated in that moment. He didn't just hate me, he hated my mother, my father, my girl friend. He was running the camp at Buchenwald, he was the Grand Inquisitor, the epitome of everyone who had ever hated the Jews.

I stomped on his back, hoping to get at his kidneys with my combat boots. I pushed him around more. I was pleased when he tried to defend himself. It gave me an excuse to hit harder. I finally backed off, my frustration and anger temporarily satisfied. He was dishevelled and dazed but he wasn't bleeding.

"I'll get you for this, Rosen," he said.

I said, "You tell anybody what I did, and I'll tell them why. I'll tell them what you've been saying, how you've been keeping my mail from me. Maybe some of these guys here will back me up."

The sergeant did find a little revenge, but it seemed minor compared to what could have happened to me. He made me guard the motor pool for thirty-six straight hours the next day, and I ended up in the hospital from exhaustion. But he never bothered me again. As a result of this incident I developed an abhorrence for violence and fighting that has stuck with me to the present day.

In those days I really believed that if you scratched a Gentile, or a "Christian," you'd find an anti-Semite. I was a Jew, militantly protective of my heritage. But if anyone had asked me to define what a Jew was at that point—and they didn't—I don't know what I would have said. Although God made the Jews distinctive by establishing covenants with Abraham and other ancient Hebrews, He seemed to have nothing to do with my own Jewishness. I fancied myself to be an agnostic and decided God probably didn't exist at all. Even if there was a God, I wanted Him to mind His own business and let me tend to mine. But I soon learned God had some ideas of His own about the matter.

3 MY SON, THE GOY

My father's belief—"religion is a racket"—made more and more sense to me as I got older. Jewish traditions might be all right, but liturgical rigmarole and irrelevant theology seemed to be all the local synagogue had to offer. I was a practical, hard-working young man, completely unspiritual. Like all good Jewish boys, I felt an intense loyalty to my family. But my ethical approach to the outside world was thoroughly pragmatic: I liked to get along with other people because life was easier that way, but I felt no particular desire to find a divine will for my life.

My lack of interest in God—and God's moral imperatives—was reinforced as I began to date my wife, Ceil. Ceil came from an Orthodox Jewish family which kept separate dishes and ate only kosher foods. But Ceil herself was a professed atheist who reacted violently against the restrictive customs that her family had imposed on her. I generally tried to observe the main fast days, such as *Yom Kippur,* the Day of Atonement, but she had nothing but contempt for such practices. I remember we were together one year on *Yom Kippur,* and though she rarely treated me to anything on our dates, she made a special point of buying me an ice-cream cone. I ate it, but felt guilty and weak because I had given in to my hunger.

Such antireligious influences didn't make me too receptive when I met my first serious Christian. He was a young man named Orville Freestone, who introduced himself to me at a Denver bus stop on *Yom Kippur* in 1949. I had just attended a service at a synagogue—out of respect for tradition, not God—and he was returning from work.

"You coming from work, too?" he asked, trying to strike up a conversation.

"No," I answered. "I spent the day in synagogue."

"Oh, you go to synagogue regularly?"

"Not really," I said. "But today is *Yom Kippur,* the Day of Atonement—a very important Jewish holiday."

"What kind of a holiday is it?"

"Well, it's the one day in the year when the Jews go to synagogue to ask for the forgiveness of sins."

"Do you feel your sins are forgiven?" he asked, pressing the conversation further than I thought comfortable.

"I hope so," I replied, and looked away, hoping he would either keep quiet or change the subject. Actually, I didn't believe there was any God to forgive sin.

"There is a way that you can know for certain that your sins are forgiven," he continued. "I know for a fact that Christ died for my sins and made it possible for me to know God and find eternal life."

"That's all right for you if it helps you and you really believe that way," I said. "But as for me, I'm a Jew."

I had only had to use that conversational ploy a couple of times in my life when I thought people were getting too pushy with their religious beliefs. It had always worked before as a conversation stopper, but not this time. Instead of keeping quiet or cowering away, Orville smiled, moved closer to me, and started shaking my hand vigorously.

"You know, I'm all the more pleased to meet you because you're Jewish," he said. "Every Jew I meet helps increase my faith in God and the Bible, because every living Jew is evidence that the God of the Bible exists and that He keeps His word."

I'm sure my mouth must have been hanging open as he spoke. I had always thought the existence of Jews was some kind of affront to Christians because we denied that He was the Messiah and had actually killed Him, according to my understanding of what Christians believed. But my silence didn't dampen Orville's enthusiasm.

"You're Jewish, and so you must know the scriptural passage that makes me feel this way," he said. "It's Genesis 12:1–3." And he proceeded to quote the verses from memory: "Now the Lord had said unto Abram, Get thee out of thy country, and from thy kindred, and from thy father's house, unto a land that I will shew thee: And I will make of thee a great nation, and I will bless thee, and make thy name great; and thou shalt be a blessing: And I will bless them that bless thee, and curse him that curseth thee: and in thee shall all families of the earth be blessed."

I was absorbed by his knowledge of the Bible and his friendliness and the apparent sincerity of his beliefs. But more than that, I was impressed that he said he believed in a glorious destiny for the Jewish people. I had never heard a Gentile say such things. He told me that one day the Jews would bear the message of redemption to all the world. Rabbis and other Jewish teachers I had heard had always seemed embarrassed by the idea of Israel as a chosen people.

Orville continued explaining his faith to me after we boarded the bus: "You see, God became a man so that He could show His love to mankind. Let me give you an illustration that someone suggested to me one time. Suppose that for some reason a man decided that he really loved the ants on a particular anthill. He began to supply them with bread and honey, but he suspected the ants didn't really understand how much he cared. If he had the power and if his love were sincere, would it make sense for him to become an ant himself for a while so that he could communicate his feelings to them?"

"I guess so," I replied with a smile. "But the love would have to be pretty strong for a man to want to become an ant."

"Exactly. And it was overwhelming love that prompted God to become a Man in Jesus Christ. He accepted the conditions and limitations of manhood so that He could show His love toward men, so He could communicate that love in a way they'd understand."

Orville gave me a pocket New Testament, and I promised to read it. After we parted at my stop, I had a lot to think about. I had fasted all day but I wasn't even aware of being hungry. I had never heard anyone explain the Christian faith so well, and I wondered if I might have to revamp my definitions of "Gentile" and "Christian."

I put the New Testament down on my dresser, lay on my bed, and stared up at the ceiling. If I read that book, I might believe it, I thought. And if I believe it, then I might believe in Christ. By believing in Christ, I will have become a Christian, according to what Orville said. And that means I will have joined the people who have persecuted us. It would amount to ethnic treason. My family would disown me, disinherit me. My friends would desert me. Other Jews would consider me a social outcast, a betrayer to my people. Who was I to make momentous decisions about things that have already been decided by our most intelligent rabbis? If all the rabbis get together and say that Jesus is the Messiah, then maybe I'll go along with them. In the meantime, it's not my problem.

I met Orville on the bus a few days later, and he tried to continue our conversation where we had left off, but I cut him short. "Look, I appreciate your concern and all, but you're not going to convert me," I said. "I really don't want to talk about this anymore."

After a couple of days, my old attitudes toward religion regained the upper hand. Religion was probably necessary to give comfort to the dying and to keep children in line. But it was still a racket for people who made their living by preaching and counseling and conducting services. The Bible, in my view—and I had read only a little of the Old and none of the New Testament at that point—was mostly nonsense. Religion was the opiate of the people. The Bible had some good moral teachings, but the supernatural events only seemed to be supernatural because people were superstitious in the old days. They needed those fairy tales because they didn't know as much as I did.

As far as I could tell, the world of religious people was far too narrow. They didn't see beauty, they didn't enjoy good literature, they didn't listen to real music. They just sang hokey hymns and read the Bible. I felt that they were basically ignorant people who needed an emotional crutch to make it through life. There was nothing unique about my view of religion, but I thought it was original and enlightened. My self-image as an open-minded liberal prevented me from seeing my own deep-rooted prejudices.

By rebuffing Orville I thought I had succeeded in pushing Christianity permanently out of my life, but I was wrong. The next spiritual onslaught came from the most unlikely source—my atheistic wife, Ceil. We had married when she was just out of high school, and I was only eighteen years old myself. But she began to show a greater sympathy for religion in general, and Christianity in particular, while she was still in school.

"The first time I remember thinking seriously about Christianity was in 1948, when my high-school music class was doing a Christmas pageant. I was one of the chorus, in long, flowing, biblical dress. We moved in a slow dance step across the stage, singing, 'Oh come, Oh come, Emmanuel, And ransom captive Israel,' " Ceil related. "I wondered if Jesus could really be the One Israel was waiting for. But then I didn't think about it again until a few years later, after we had been married for a year. It was the Christmas of 1951, and I was sitting at home listening to Christmas carols. Again, the words of a song, this time "O Little Town of Bethlehem,' raised the same question in my mind. I prayed and said, 'God, would You show me what is the right way? Is there anything to what they're saying about Jesus? Is Christianity true? If it is, I'd like to know about it. Otherwise, I'll go back to Judaism, if You show me that I should. Please show me what's true!' "

Ceil said that she temporarily forgot about this conversation with God, and she certainly never told me about it. I would have laughed her out of the house. After all, she had encouraged me to break a *Yom Kippur* fast several years before. But a few days later, after we came home late from a wedding, she went off by herself and looked out one of our windows at the sky.

"I saw this star shining down at me, and it looked exceptionally huge," she said. "I wondered, could that be what the Bethlehem star looked like? The words to the Christmas carol came to mind again, and I found myself sort of believing it. It was a kind of emotional experience for me at the time. Each day after that I found myself believing a little bit more, and a little bit more. I felt a pull, a tugging from somewhere inside me to know more about Christianity. It just kept growing in me."

Ceil found herself wanting to read the New Testament, but she was afraid to buy one because her mother, who lived right up the street, wouldn't have stood for it. She finally got up the courage a few months later to ask a cousin to pick up a cheap Bible in a local dime store. She knew better than to ask me, of course.

"I felt sheepish about it," Ceil explained. "I was chicken, but I was dying to read it. And as I got further into the Gospels, it was as though I had finally come home. I thought, 'Why don't we believe this? It's so reasonable. Here Jesus is, quoting Jewish Scriptures and prophecies.' The whole thing made sense to me. I thought it was beautiful. The person of Jesus seemed so real. When I reached the end of the Gospels, I was actually disappointed because the story was finished."

Her excitement was such that she finally couldn't contain herself. She began to say to me, "Do you know it says such and such in the New Testament?" But I wasn't interested. I was doing well as a salesman in a sporting-goods store and was studying business at a local college. My life was reasonably well-ordered, and I didn't need any *bobbe-myseh,* or old wives' tale, to foul things up for me.

"I was well on my way to becoming a Christian at that point, and I wanted to have someone to talk to about the things I was learning," Ceil remembers. "I had met Orville Freestone through Moishe, and so I decided to try to get in touch with him and his wife, but I learned they had moved out of town. That was disappointing. But then I decided to try prayer again. I had asked God to show me whether Jesus was the Messiah, and I seemed to be getting some answers. So I asked Him to help me find somebody to talk to. Soon afterwards—this was early in 1953—a Hebrew-Christian missionary, Hannah Wago, came to our door. No one, as far as I knew, was aware of my need to talk to this woman. It was such a fantastic experience that I went back to the pantry to cry, because I didn't want her to see me. Her arrival was a real answer to prayer. The next Sunday—it was Easter—I went to a Baptist church which the missionary suggested to me. I walked forward at the minister's invitation and publicly professed my faith in Christ."

I told Ceil it was all right with me if she wanted to go to church once in a while, but I didn't want her to make a regular thing out of it. The whole business seemed to me to be getting out of hand, and I was getting a little annoyed. It was a lot of nonsense, in my view, sure to lead to trouble with relatives, employers, and friends. Besides, who wanted to be associated with a bunch of religious fanatics?

Because I was proud of my own liberalism, I hesitated to show my irritation to Ceil. Her religious interest could have been a fad, like an obsession for canasta that she had just experienced. But I knew she was a bright girl, unlikely to equate a serious religious commitment with a card game. My attitude toward her grew more and more intolerant.

I said, "Okay, so you believe it in your heart, but don't tell anybody, don't go to church, and our baby will have to be raised Jewish." Sometimes, after one of our conversations, I secretly suspected that her view of Christianity made sense, but then I always considered such thoughts to be a false alarm. Finally, I decided that I was getting tired of being barraged with all this spiritual nonsense, and I told her I didn't want her to talk to Mrs. Wago, the missionary. The next day, I came home and found Ceil listening on the phone, discussing a Bible lesson. There was only one thing I could do, given my state of mind at the time: I ripped the telephone out of the wall by the roots.

Ceil was embarrassed, but she remained surprisingly sweet. She said, "I love you, but please don't make me choose between Jesus and you." I was in agony. I didn't know what to do with her. As a last resort, I downed a couple of double shots of whiskey and went over to see my father. Ordinarily I kept liquor in the house only for guests, but I needed to do something to give me the courage to discuss such an unpleasant topic.

"Dad, I have a real problem," I began. "Ceil says she believes in Jesus. She reads the New Testament, she prays. I don't think she's flipped, but I don't see how I can live with her when she's going on like this. Do you think we should get a divorce?"

"Shame on you," my father said, ignoring the question. "You've been drinking."

"You know I usually don't drink. It's just that I'm worried."

"You can't be serious about divorcing her. She's a nice Jewish girl, from a nice family. You shouldn't drink if you make such silly jokes."

We didn't really get anywhere in our conversation because I didn't know exactly how to explain my predicament. I didn't tell my father Ceil was a Christian, because to me that meant being a church member and she had never joined any church. In fact, she had honored my demand that she not attend church.

But when I returned home, I found the situation unchanged. She left booklets lying around, some of them on absurd topics like heaven. I thought one of them was utterly laughable, with descriptions of streets of gold, pearly gates, and other *goyish*, or gentile, superstitions. But as silly as those pamphlets seemed, they started me thinking: Heaven can't be like that, I decided, but then I realized I was assuming that there might be a heaven. If there was, what was it like?

A few days later, on a Saturday evening, I was sitting in my favorite chair, and I found myself asking, "What do I really believe?" I suddenly realized that it might all be true. That was an awesome moment. Many Jews reach that point. They believe it just might be true. Faith grows slowly; it creeps up on you. When I looked inside myself, I realized I actually believed what my wife had been saying, and I didn't know what to do next. It was scary. I told Ceil, and she started throwing Bible verses at me. We began to pray. Kneeling had always been out of the question for me, because it had seemed such a gentile custom. But we actually knelt at our bed that evening. By then I was so devastated inside that I would have done anything. If she had said, "Stand on your head and pray," I would have stood on my head and prayed. I was completely pliable and had lost all my bearings at that point. Five minutes before, I had possessed a coherent, secular-Jewish philosophy of life. Now, that was all in the past. I had known who I was, what I wanted, where I was going, but now I was like a baby that needed to be taught everything from the beginning.

We went to church the next morning—it was Pentecost Sunday of 1953—and I went forward and professed my faith publicly, as Ceil had done on Easter Sunday. My whole outlook on life changed drastically after that. If Jesus was really the Promised One, the Messiah —and I believed deeply now that He was—then it seemed important for me to learn all about Him as quickly as possible and model my life after His.

The only spiritual authority I knew, outside of the Bible, was the church, so I took everything my new minister said very seriously. All he had to do was to drop a hint that the members of the congregation should do this or that, and I'd try. We went to Sunday school, church, the Baptist Training Union on Sunday afternoons, and the evening service. The pastor suggested that more people should be attending the Wednesday night prayer meetings, and I arranged my hours at the sporting-goods store so that I could comply. When they had a deacons' meeting, he would announce that other members of the church were also welcome, and I would take him at his word and show up for that. It took me a while to find that other Christians didn't take all these admonitions and suggestions so seriously.

My first few church services revealed an entirely new world. The music, for example, was radically different from chanting in the synagogue. All the hymns had a lilt to them, and I wasn't accustomed to Christian symbolism. They sang, "There is a fountain filled with blood drawn from Immanuel's veins; And sinners, plunged beneath that flood, lose all their guilty stains." The cheerful lilting melody seemed so unsuited to the graphically violent lyrics. And I didn't know who Immanuel was, but the poor guy seemed to be making a big contribution to the blood bank. I was as accepting as I could be, but it wasn't easy. Then I noticed there was an item in the church bulletin: NEXT SUNDAY: COMMUNION.

An usher in the last row had told us when we arrived the first morning that if we needed any help, we should feel free to call on him. I think he was just being polite because, as I learned later, church services involve very little conversation among the listeners. The synagogue is much noisier. Even gossip during prayers is sanctified according to the Talmud. I also had to learn not to get up and walk around because Jewish tradition permits the congregation to enter and leave at will during the three-hour synagogue services.

So, not knowing any better, I said, "Psst!" in a rather loud tone and motioned the usher over. "What does it mean, 'Communion'?" I asked.

"You're Jewish, right?" he answered. "It's a little like a Passover feast."

My eyes must have lit up at that. The Passover Seder usually involved a rather painless religious observance and then a huge repast. In my grandfather's house we traditionally started with chopped liver (and onions), hard-boiled eggs (and onions), pickled herring (and onions), and matzo-ball soup. Those were just appetizers. Next came the roast meats—poultry, kid, and lamb. And finally we had several kinds of dessert, including honey cake, sponge cake, and macaroons. Communion sounded terrific to me.

"How much does it cost?" I asked.

"It doesn't cost you anything," he replied. "You just contribute anything you want to in the church collection plate."

That was a great improvement over the synagogue, where we had to buy tickets for most of the big events, including the major holiday services, and also were assessed a regular yearly membership fee. The bulletin said, "Prepare your hearts for Communion next Sunday," and so I asked, "Should I do anything to help out, maybe bring something?"

"No, it's all provided," he said.

"Where will it be held?"

"Right here in the sanctuary."

I looked around at the old oak pews but didn't see much space for tables. TV trays had just come into vogue, and I thought maybe they'd fix the place up with a few of those.

Ceil and I ate a very small breakfast the next Sunday because of the huge meal we expected at the service. I sought out the usher during Sunday school and double-checked with him about the time and place, because I didn't want to miss anything. I suspected that, being Gentiles, they would serve bacon and ham and shrimp and other things that weren't kosher, but it still seemed like a nice idea, a real treat.

Ceil and I got seated in the sanctuary, and we began to sing songs about the blood again:

> Oh! Precious is the flow
> That makes me white as snow;
> No other fount I know,
> Nothing but the blood of Jesus.
> —ROBERT LOWRY

That wasn't too appetizing, especially since I didn't understand the real import of the words. But to top it all off, when I looked up at the front of the church, I saw on a table what looked like white shrouds, with a lump where the feet would be and another lump for the head. I thought, "Gee, they're having a funeral today, too." It made perfect sense to me that they'd be having a funeral that morning because their customs were so different from what I had known. But up to that point I hadn't seen a dead body, and I had the usual terror of such things. And what did the pastor preach on? The body and blood of Christ: eating and drinking it.

I hate to tell you the thoughts that were going through my mind. I knew they couldn't have Christ up there under that shroud. And I knew deep down that these *goyim* weren't cannibals. I decided the body was probably just being kept there, and they would have the funeral later that afternoon.

"Psst!" I said and motioned my friend, the usher, over. "When are we going to have Communion? I'm losing my appetite a little bit."

Straining to be patient, he said, "It'll be in just a minute."

At the end of the service eight men dressed in dark suits went forward toward the shrouds. I didn't know the difference between deacons and other church officials at that point, and so I decided they were the pallbearers. They gathered around what I assumed to be the funeral bier, and I expected they would carry the body out before we ate. But two of them moved to each end of the covered object, and I could see they were waiting for a signal to lift the shroud. Oh, no, I thought. Suddenly the cover fell away, and there was nothing underneath except some little pots and pans.

"Psst! What's that?"

"Communion."

Communion! I looked around and saw there were about three hundred people to feed. I was totally dumbfounded. After certain prayers were said, each person was given a crumb of matzo. Then there were some more prayers, and a blessing was offered over the wine. Finally, the deacons passed around little glass thimbles filled with what looked like wine. But when I drank it, yech, it was grape juice! I couldn't understand why they called it wine, and by now I was getting impatient.

"Psst!" I said to my usher. "When are we going to have Communion?"

"You've had it," he replied.

I thought, boy, these *goyim,* they give you a crumb of matzo and a thimbleful of grape juice, and they have the nerve to call it a Passover feast. Then they criticize us Jews for being stingy!

Getting accustomed to Christian practices and customs was not the easiest thing for me, but I learned little by little. I was used to liturgical Hebrew prayers which always began, *"Baruch ata Adonai. Elohenu melech ha-olam asher . . ."* or, "Praised be thou, O Lord our God, King of the Universe . . . ." I noticed several people in the Baptist church started their prayers with, "Dear gracious heavenly Father, we come unto you . . . ." That must be the Christian formula, I decided, and so I memorized it. It was much easier than the synagogue service because everything in church was in English. But imagine my shock when someone dared to change the introductory prayer phrase at the next service!

It was as though I had entered a strange new civilization, another planet, and had to learn all my traditions and values from scratch again. But it was enjoyable in a way because I believed Christ had died for me and had given me an access to God that I had always considered impossible. What was not so enjoyable was trying to explain my newfound faith to my parents.

My method for informing them about my spiritual experience was thoroughly ill-conceived. I called a family meeting and waited until everyone was seated before I spoke.

"I've been studying the Bible lately, and I've decided that Jesus is really the Messiah," I began. "We've all been wrong, and I wanted you to know that I'm going to believe in Him and follow Him and give my life to Him."

"What, you crazy?" my father growled. "First you come over making a joke about Ceil, now this. What's going on?"

"No, I really mean this," I replied. "We've all been misled in rejecting Jesus all these years. I really believe that."

My father is a proud man, and staging such an abrasive confrontation in his own home must have humiliated him. At any rate, he certainly got angry.

"You can just get out of my house!" he shouted. "And don't come back until you've given up this Jesus business!"

My life as their son the Christian, the social outcast and traitor to his people, had started more spectacularly than even I had expected.

4 THE JEW FIRST

The young man sported a *yarmulkah* and had a wild look in his eye as he barrelled toward me. I sat calmly at the Hebrew-Christian information desk in the Beth Sar Shalom building lobby and glanced over my shoulder to see whom he was after. There was no one in sight but me. Before I could focus in on him again, he had reached my booth. Shouting a curse, he scattered all my literature—thousands of small tracts and pamphlets—to the floor with one sweep of his arm. He turned and dashed out before I realized what had happened.

I had only been a Christian for a short time and I thought manning the desk for a few evenings a week would be a quiet, easy way to get used to serving the Lord. As I recovered from the shock of the encounter, I wearily got up and began the arduous task of sorting all the pamphlets into their respective piles again. I couldn't figure it out at first. I had been sitting there quietly, minding my own business. The whole incident made me a little angry as I mulled it over, but then I remembered Jesus' teachings about loving my enemies and rejoicing when men persecuted and cursed me. This must be God's way of testing and teaching me, I decided. Just an isolated incident to show me how hostile some Jews could be to the gospel.

But the harassment wasn't as isolated as I had hoped. The same fellow came in the next day and the next. I found I could expect him several times a week for the next couple of weeks. Other than his curses, there was no real communication between us. As I got up to gather the scattered pamphlets after each attack, I rationalized by saying, "Well, at least they won't get dusty this way. Nobody else seems interested in touching them."

Finally, the young fellow, whose name turned out to be Jeff, surprised me by asking a question.

"Why are you doing this?" he asked.

"I believe that Jesus is the Messiah," I replied. "Do you know anything about Bible prophecy?"

"I am a disciple of one of the Hasidic rabbis, and so I know something about it," he said.

I then proceeded to show him some verses from the Old Testament, but before I could finish, he cried, "I can't stand it, I can't stand it!" and he kicked over my chair and knocked over the table and ran out again.

I thought I had heard the last of this wild man, but two years later a letter from Jeff was forwarded to me. "Praise the Lord!" it began. "Jesus came into my life after He had struggled with me all those years. I was so angry that I think if I had met Him on the street, I would have spit at Him. But He kept talking to me, and now I know He's who He claimed to be. My life is as completely dedicated to serving Him now as it was to fighting Him before."

That experience taught me a lot about myself and about evangelism among the Jews. I myself had resisted and resisted God, and then I became equally zealous on His side. But I had never observed those same tendencies so clearly in another Jew. Most Jews are indifferent, apathetic to spiritual matters, and those, for me, are the most difficult people with whom to communicate. I sometimes prefer to encounter anti-Christian zealots because they seem to care deeply and to have the most potential to do God's work. The Apostle Paul did a complete, enthusiastic turnabout. So did Jeff. And so did I. There is every reason to think other Jews would react in the same way.

I have my own definition of a fanatic: A fanatic is anyone who feels as strongly about anything as I do about Jesus. There is only one central focus in my life: Jesus is Lord, the risen Lord and Messiah. Sometimes I have to find a diversion because of the overwhelming sense of awe I feel for the Lordship of Christ. I have an inner compulsion to get out and tell people what I know to be the truth.

From the beginning, my desire to spread the gospel among the Jews was reinforced by what the Apostle Paul said in Romans 1:16: "For I am not ashamed of the gospel of Christ; for it is the power of God unto salvation to every one that believeth; *to the Jew first,* and also to the Greek" (emphasis supplied). I identify with that statement completely. It's a battle cry that has echoed inside me from the earliest days of my Christian experience.

But I ran into two major problems immediately after my acceptance of Jesus as the Messiah. My personal study of the Scriptures didn't give me the depth of Bible knowledge that I craved. And a new job had isolated me almost entirely from the people I most wanted to talk to—the Jews. My new position was sales manager of a Denver cemetery, and the pay was quite lucrative. But I had little contact with customers myself, and the people I did meet were not Jews, because Jews traditionally buried their dead in special cemeteries reserved for Jews alone.

I felt inadequate and dissatisfied, so I asked God what I should do. A friend of mine had said to me, "You shouldn't pray for God to send laborers to the harvest. Your first prayer should be, 'Lord, do you want me to be a laborer, a minister of the gospel?' "

The point got through, but my attitude was rather negative: "Lord, you don't want me, do you? I'm not good enough, and I don't want to be any better."

Then one day I was reading the Bible in church, thinking and praying about my future, and I noticed a passage from Acts 20:21. Paul told the elders of the church at Ephesus that he had been "Testifying both to the Jews and also to the Greeks, repentance toward God, and faith toward our Lord Jesus Christ." That verse might not have meant anything special to anyone else, but to me it was a unique spiritual experience. God was saying, "Moishe Rosen, I want you." That was it. I often have prayers answered like that. I pray, and search the Scriptures, and God draws my eye to a particular passage. A spiritual connection develops between my own mind and God's Word, and I receive an insight, a firm conviction. I immediately realized that God was speaking to me, showing me His will.

All doubts left my mind after that. I knew that God wanted me. He was issuing an imperative, and it was up to me to start looking into how I could help bring it about. I had some money tied up in the family business and also in my cemetery job, and so I started planning. At the suggestion of officials at the Beth Sar Shalom Fellowship in New York, which is sponsored by the American Board of Missions to the Jews, I enrolled at Northeastern Bible College in New Jersey. But before I left, I began to pray that things could get straightened out between me and my family.

Both my mother and father had disowned me for the better part of the year that followed my announcement to them of my decision to follow Jesus. Eleven months had passed, and no one in my family would talk to me. Jewish people who had been my friends shunned me. I really learned the meaning of the Christian's relatives becoming his "foes," but the Lord took care of my needs by giving me the strength to bear the rejection.

Finally, in an apparent answer to my prayers, my brother Don called and said, "Look, Dad wants to get together with you. Is it all right if I come over and discuss things with you and our rabbi?"

I agreed, and we set up a time. Through Don's and the rabbi's efforts, my dad and I finally got together the next week, and I was almost sorry I had to give him some more bad news about my decision to enter the ministry.

"Look, I'm glad we're on speaking terms again, but I'm worried about you," my father said. "I wonder—and I don't want you to get upset—but I wonder if you haven't cracked up altogether. Just do one thing for me. Before you leave here and get too far away for anyone to take care of you, go to see a psychiatrist. Find a good Christian doctor, but do it, just for my peace of mind. I'll pay for it. You could go away and crack up and there wouldn't be anyone to take care of your wife and the baby."

Our first daughter, Lyn, had been born by this time, and Dad was genuinely worried about her and Ceil. I agreed to go along with his suggestion because, frankly, I thought there was always the possibility that I might really be insane. I didn't know anything about psychiatrists, but I had noticed the name of one in a local news article, and so I called his office.

"Is it possible, do you think that a sane Jew could believe that Jesus is the Messiah?" I asked him on the phone.

"It's possible," he said. So the next day I found myself lying nervously on his fake-leather couch, staring at the ceiling as the doctor's voice came to me from behind his desk across the room.

He was a short man with a receding hairline, a large nose, and watery little eyes.

"Well, and what brings you here?" he began.

"My father wanted me to come. I have become a believer in Jesus, and lately I have felt the hand of God guiding me . . . ."

At that he arose from his desk and came over to the couch. He peered at me intently, not quite able to hide a new glint of interest in his eyes.

"Tell me, Martin," he asked too gently, "just where upon your body do you feel the hand of God?"

I sat up with a start as a cold, hot, prickly feeling started in my scalp and ran over my entire body. At that moment I learned a quick lesson which has affected my ministry ever since: I learned to avoid religious jargon whenever possible. "No, no," I hastened to explain. "That's idiomatic. I didn't feel the hand of God physically. It just means I had an inner conviction."

He then began to ask me a lot of questions about my sex life, but how much of a sex life could I have had? I got married when I was eighteen and spent all my spare time until then working and going to school. I'm afraid my sex life was very dull. He dropped that subject and began telling me what he didn't believe about God.

Remembering that his fee was fifty dollars an hour, I stopped him. "Just a minute," I said. "I really enjoy talking to you, but one thing

I want to know—when you're talking to me, is my father paying for the time?"

He gave a start and turned red.

"I don't want to be rude," I continued, "and I do think your opinions are interesting, but I don't think it's worth fifty dollars an hour for me to sit here and listen."

He then became very professional, tested my reflexes, and asked a few more questions. After the second session he told me that was enough. He evidently told my father I was sane, and I received a letter from him several weeks later. It said, "To whom it may concern: Martin Rosen . . . was examined psychiatrically by the undersigned on August 2 and 3, 1954. He was found to be psychiatrically normal."

So no matter what anyone says about my mental stability these days, I at least have a letter to prove it. Most people don't.

Ceil, our two-year-old daughter, Lyn, and I left for New Jersey soon afterwards, but it took a while for us to adjust to the academic environment. Because we were accustomed to Jewish-style cooking, we had little appetite for the *goyish* dormitory dining-room fare. We would take garlic powder and red peppers to every meal in an effort to make the food palatable.

I also had some special personal problems that kept me occupied. As I mentioned earlier, I had trouble during the early days of my new faith, because I took everything that pastors and more experienced Christians said too seriously. I sometimes think that ministers are given to overstatement because they believe if they exaggerate, they may get their listeners to go along with them at least halfway. But not me. Christianity was an all-or-nothing proposition for me, and that meant following to the letter every admonition and suggestion that came from the lips of those in authority.

Because of my literal-mindedness, the Bible college almost ruined me during my first month of study. During the first week, we heard a special speaker who expounded on the virtues of Bible reading.

"You must recognize that the Bible is God's Word, and that means you should read it as a love letter from the Lord for an hour each day!" he said.

I was taking several Bible courses, but I decided to try his suggestion. I got up an hour earlier, and I can honestly say that it was worth it. But my newfound Christian responsibilities didn't stop there. Our next special speaker spoke on prayer.

"God loves you, and you should love God," he stressed. "But how can you love God if you don't communicate through long talks with Him? Each of you should be spending at least an hour each day in prayer."

I had never spent more than ten consecutive minutes in prayer. But he suggested getting up an hour earlier to pray, and I resolved to do it, even though the sun was barely up when I arose to fulfill my new spiritual obligations.

But I wasn't finished yet. The next week, another speaker arrived to give his views on witnessing to non-Christians.

"No serious Christians can escape the command that Jesus gave us in the Great Commission, that we must spread the gospel throughout the world," he said. "I know of one great man who would not go to sleep at night until he had received an answer to a fervent daily prayer that God would give him at least one soul to witness to."

Because an inner need to witness and evangelize had been a major force in my considering the ministry, I decided that I would devote some time each evening to looking for spiritually hungry people. I wandered around the streets, looking for pedestrians who might respond to the gospel. If I saw someone who was waiting for a bus, or perhaps just loitering, I would walk over and with my best Dale Carnegie smile, exclaim, "How are you this evening?" I soon found that people didn't respond too well to that approach. After a couple of nights of pounding the streets, I consistently found myself at about 2 A.M. in the local bus station, waiting for someone to arrive so that I could give my daily witness and go home. I was tired and unhappy, and I shuffled through textbooks on the bus bench without really studying.

"There's something wrong with me," I finally muttered. "I'm awful; I must be rotten. I don't want to pray or read the Bible. I just want to go to bed."

It seemed to me that if I were really spiritual it wouldn't matter that I was getting only four hours of sleep a night.

At that moment, it seemed as though God reached down and patted me on the head and said, "Don't worry about it, Moishe. You don't have to try so hard to grow. You'll grow naturally. Just take it easy."

Relieved, I immediately returned home. After that I resisted attempts to manipulate me, to force piety into my personality. I became my own man, spiritually speaking. While I continued to listen closely to the advice of more experienced Christians, I learned that the ultimate spiritual authority in my life had to rest in my relationship to God through prayer and in His written Word.

On my graduation from Bible college, I was firmly committed to a
ministry with the American Board of Missions to the Jews. Dr. Daniel
Fuchs, the executive director of the board, decided that I would be
best suited to take over the work in Los Angeles. Though I had wanted
that assignment, I was overwhelmed at the thought of the responsibility. It would be just me and my faith in God against California.

I had never been west of Denver, and when I arrived in Los Angeles
my first impression seemed justified—I felt totally inadequate to
handle the job. There were so many Jews, and I was so inexperienced.
I thought, "Rosen, maybe you'd better just go back to Denver and
become a salesman again. Witness a little on the side, be a good lay-
man, but don't get yourself in a situation like this, where you're over
your head." But then I remembered all the answered prayers, all the
"boot camp" training at the Bible college. I was determined that if
God had gotten me this far, He could carry me the rest of the way.

My main problem on our arrival in California was finding a point
at which to start. My objective was to establish a foothold for Jewish
evangelism, and in effect I had to start from scratch. The American
Board had purchased a small house in a Jewish section of Los Angeles
for our headquarters, and we moved our meager belongings into an
upstairs room. The lower section of the house had been remodeled
into a meeting room. I was only getting paid $200 a month when we
arrived there in 1957, so we couldn't afford a larger place for ourselves. The room was a little crowded because by then we had another
daughter, Ruth, who was a year old.

My early years had been spent in Jewish neighborhoods, but I had
never lived in a Jewish district with the sole intention of spreading the
gospel to the other residents. As we were unpacking and moving our
things into the house, I was thinking and praying about how to
approach the neighborhood. Before I could formulate a plan, my six-
year-old daughter, Lyn, showed up with a little girl who apparently
had been making mud pies all day, and her older brother, who presented an immaculate contrast with his scrubbed face and spotless
white shirt.

I was happy that Lyn had found some playmates, but I was a little
sad, too. I knew it would just be a matter of time until their parents
found out we were Jews who believed in Jesus. That would be hard
on Lyn and Ruth, I thought. As I was pondering this problem, their
mother appeared.

She walked right up to me and in broken English introduced herself
as Mrs. Cohen, a Jew who had immigrated from Holland. Without

giving me a chance to respond, she said, "You are Jewish and you believe in . . . Yayzus?"

I knew she meant "Jesus," and my heart sank.

"Yes," I replied. I was almost wishing Lyn had kept her mouth shut about our beliefs for a day or two.

"But you are Jewish," she said.

"That's right," I responded. Well, here it comes, I thought. We're about to get lambasted.

"And you are . . . like a domine, a minister?"

"Yes." I knew I didn't look much like a minister, because at the time I wasn't wearing a tie. Because of my own image of a minister, I always wore a suit and tie in those days.

"I've been looking for you," she said. "I wanted someone to tell me about Yayzus."

I thought she was telling me she was angry because she had such a serious, almost pained expression on her face. But through a combination of English, Yiddish, and sign language I learned that she had been praying that God would show her the truth about Jesus. During the next few days Ceil continued to communicate with her through Bible verses, by comparing the Dutch Bible with the English Bible. In the meantime, I sent a postcard to Dr. Elias den Arend, a nearby Hebrew-Christian missionary from Holland, to see if he could visit her. Before my postcard had a chance to reach this man, he and his wife appeared at my doorstep. He explained that he felt God had led him to drop in on us to see if we needed help. That afternoon, this missionary and his Dutch wife spent several hours with Mrs. Cohen and her husband, and finally all four of them bowed their heads. Even if I didn't know their language, I knew what was happening. The Cohens became our first believers. I didn't even have time to sit down and plan a missionary strategy because things just started happening.

The Cohens' commitment to Christ was God's answer to my lack of faith and my uncertainty. I was ready to be cursed, to have things thrown in our yard, to be snubbed by all the neighbors. Instead, the neighborhood received us well, and most of the kids who lived near us started coming to our Bible study.

During the ten years we lived in Los Angeles, God brought scores of Jewish inquirers into our mission services, and He even provided a spacious new mission headquarters in Hollywood. I learned to communicate the gospel on an individual level to every imaginable kind of Jewish person during that period—children, adolescents, middle-aged businessmen, and social misfits. But perhaps the greatest challenge I faced was trying to preach effectively to hostile street crowds.

5 HECKLERS, SCHMECKLERS!

As a new Christian, I was a reserved, rather shy person who preferred to deal with people on an individual level rather than in groups. The idea of speaking to an audience petrified me because of a tendency I have to stammer.

This behind-the-scenes mentality was reflected in the volunteer work I did during my Bible-school days for the Beth Sar Shalom Fellowship in New York City. I naturally gravitated toward the janitorial work. Pushing a broom and passing out hymnals were good enough for me because I had no desire to shoulder any responsibility that would thrust me into the public eye.

But one day the executive secretary, Harold Pretlove, called me into his office and announced, "I think we have a ministry for you."

I hoped they didn't want me to teach anything, because I felt rather inadequate with only a few months of Bible-school training under my belt. But before I could say anything, he continued, "We think it would be good for you to start conducting some outdoor meetings."

"What's an outdoor meeting?" I queried.

"You find a street corner, set up a platform, and begin speaking."

"Whom do I speak to?" I asked.

"To whomever you can get to listen," he replied with a smile.

Then I realized what he was saying! I was horrified! I hardly had enough nerve to give my testimony in a small group. But I was afraid to show him how gutless I was, and so I accepted. He told me to make an announcement to the congregation the next Sunday so that I could get someone to help me. I only hoped someone more experienced than I would volunteer. My spirits fell as my volunteers appeared the next Sunday. There was one seventy-year-old lady, Mrs. Anna Frank, whose upper denture fell down when she got excited, and there was a sixty-seven-year-old-man who was completely deaf. Finally, there was a middle-aged woman who had had a little Bible-college training. These were the three who were supposed to help me preach.

We arranged to meet at the corner of Seventy-third and Broadway, on Manhattan's upper West Side, the following Sunday afternoon. As I walked toward the appointed spot a week later, I felt as though I were heading toward a hangman's noose. It was the worst thing that I could have imagined happening to me. I recalled one street preacher in Denver who wore a clerical collar and had a remote stare as he stood there singing hymns without any accompaniment. Before I became a Christian, I had always thought the guy was a real fanatic and had looked down on him as a weird specimen. He would stand in front of The May Company department store and testify every Sunday afternoon. I felt a grudging admiration for his courage, but I was embarrassed for him because it all seemed so futile when nobody stopped to listen. Now, I seemed to be going the same route.

I knew I'd have to stand up and talk to the wind, but as humiliating as that was, I wondered what I would do if someone actually stopped and listened to me. I had prepared a theological discourse on all the messianic passages and was reviewing the speech in my mind when I reached the corner and joined the others. The first thing I did, after surveying the surrounding territory, was to pick an isolated traffic island which almost no pedestrians used. I set up a portable platform, and Mrs. Frank, with her loose uppers, stepped up on it and gave a clickety-click testimony. She spoke in English and Yiddish, and I got so involved in what she was saying that I lost a little of my fear. Then the old man got up and said, "I don't have much to say. I just got saved, two years, and I praise the Lord. I got saved because my daughter Florence was saved. She's going to talk now." Then the middle-aged woman got up and said a few things and finally it was my turn.

I had written my speech on school notebook paper, and I read it as though I were delivering a proclamation. Nobody at all walked by in the forty-five minutes we were out there, and I was relieved when it was over. I thanked God for our lack of listeners and wondered if I could legitimately call myself a failure and turn future street-corner assignments over to someone else who would do a better job.

But Mrs. Frank interrupted my thoughts: "Brother Rosen, you know you had such a nice message prepared. You're going to be a theologian. I know you're young, but you're going to be a good preacher. But you know what I think?"

"No, what, Mrs. Frank?"

"I think it would be nice if next week we had our outdoor meeting at a spot where somebody could hear us."

That settled it. I didn't dare back out now, and from then on I preached on some street corner every Sunday with these faithful three. We'd sometimes have fifty or sixty people listening to us.

My street preaching continued for the entire three years that I was in Bible college, and I developed some skill at it. I watched other street preachers, studied what made them successful or unsuccessful in holding the attention of an audience, and began to develop some techniques of my own. During the summers, I would carry my portable pulpit on the subway with a supply of tracts and preach on Wall Street daily during the lunch hours. The wonder of it all was that I drew a crowd every day.

The biggest problem I faced, and one of the most useful for my later work, was the challenge posed by hecklers. There were always several onlookers who wanted to get in on the act, too, and so there was ample opportunity to develop an ability at repartee and spirited dialogue as well as straight oratory. I usually found that the heckler helped to build up the crowd, and once the crowd got large enough, I started hitting them with my message.

One day, for example, I was preaching on the Son of God. An older man who was walking past called out, "God doesn't have a Son!"

"Did you say God doesn't have a Son?" I asked.

"That's right," he retorted, stopping at my challenge.

"Then how come I believe it?" I said. I knew this was not a logical question, but I was just interested in engaging him in an interchange.

"Because you're stupid," he replied, drawing a laugh from the growing crowd of onlookers.

"It seems to me it says so some place in the Bible," I said.

"In your Bible, maybe, but not in mine. I'm a Jew." He moved in closer as I looked a little crestfallen. "If you can find a place in the Bible where it says God has a Son—I mean in the *real* Bible, not the New Testament—then I'll convert and preach your religion myself."

At this point he apparently thought I was trying to avoid the issue, so he turned up the volume of his voice: "If you can show me in the Jewish Bible where it says that God had a Son, then I'll convert and be like you!"

"In the Jewish Bible?" I asked meekly.

"Yeah."

"Do you have a Jewish Bible with you?" I asked.

"Do I look stupid, that I should carry a Bible around like you?"

"I've got a Jewish Bible," I replied, pulling it out of my briefcase. I opened it up to the Book of Proverbs, and by then we were getting so much attention that the crowd had boxed him in. The Bible was in English, but I asked him, "Can you read?"

"Of course I can read," he said.

"Well, you sound like a Hebrew scholar, but I wasn't so sure if you could read English," I said.

"Well, I can read fine."

I then turned to Proverbs 30:4 in the Masoretic text and covered the lower part of the verse with my hand. "Okay, read it," I said.

He looked over my arm and began to read, " 'Who hath ascended up into heaven and descended?' "

"Now that's God, right?" I asked.

"Okay. Let me finish. 'Who hath gathered the wind in his fists?' That's God, not the Son of God."

"Keep going," I prodded.

" 'Who hath bound the waters in his garment?' "

"Now that's poetry, it just means . . . ."

"Okay, okay, that's God," he said. " 'Who hath established all the ends of the earth?' That's God! God! God!"

"Keep reading," I said.

" 'What is his name?' Not Jesus! It's *Adonai* [the Hebrew name for God]!"

"Read it louder," I said.

" 'And what is his son's name, if thou knowest . . . .' "

His voice was dropping, and at that point I took over and began to preach. I didn't call on him to convert, of course, and he slunk away quietly. I had acquired a tremendous crowd by baiting him into a discussion and then using his opposition as a springboard for my sermon on Jesus as the Son of God.

Street crowds usually gather about fifty or a hundred feet away, where they can hear but still not be too close. One day a short Jewish guy stood directly in front of my platform with his face not three feet from mine, in front of fifteen or so listeners, and started staring directly up at the skyscrapers overhead. He was what is known in the trade as a silent heckler—one of the toughest for a speaker to handle effectively. It wasn't long before that nut had everybody in the crowd staring up, trying to see what he was looking at, and I had completely lost their attention. But God sent the answer to me like a thunderbolt. The passage in Acts 1:11 came to my mind. I flipped over to it in my Bible and began to read loudly, "Ye men of Galilee, why stand ye gazing up into heaven? this same Jesus, which is taken up from you into heaven, shall so come in like manner as ye have seen him go into heaven."

The crowd was with me now, smiling, and even the silent heckler was grinning. I launched into a sermon on the Second Coming, and had one of the most attentive audiences I've ever encountered at a street meeting. I invited the heckler out to have coffee with me afterwards and told him he really had me stymied until, in my opinion, God stepped in.

After we moved to Los Angeles, I continued to do outdoor speaking in the public parks. Because I was a Jew advocating Christianity, I managed to draw a variety of Jewish listeners who had peculiar talents for needling me. Jewish hecklers are like Jews in practically every other field of endeavor. They always want to be the best. Their heckling is not usually vicious. They do it for sport.

Perhaps the worst (or best) was a frustrated opera singer who had done some singing as a cantor in a synagogue. Every time I stood up to speak, he would stand in front of me and sing at the top of his voice. He was an Italian Jew who came to Hollywood because he thought he could make it big in the movies. I thought I could outlast him by continuing to talk, but he had such incredible endurance that I didn't have a chance. I couldn't even hear myself. I wanted to preach the gospel more than anything else, so I kept trying for two or three Sunday afternoons in a row, but to no avail. I learned that his name was Moishe, too, and I began to wonder how I could appeal to him in terms he would understand.

Finally, I took him aside after one of those fruitless sessions and said, "I know you don't agree with what I say, Moishe, but for me this is a living. I'm paid for preaching. If I can't do it, if I fail, they'll fire me. I have a wife and two children. Let me preach. Let me do my work."

Now this argument was substantially true; preaching was my living, and if I failed, my superiors might possibly have fired me, I suppose, though I don't think they would have fired me just for ineffectual sermons in the park. But knowing that he was Jewish, and being a Jew myself, I felt that the best way to make him understand my plight was to make a plea for my job. Most Jews will respect an argument like that. You don't take bread out of anybody's mouth. It's a terrible thing, to take away a man's living.

Moishe not only agreed to let me preach, but he became a friend. He wasn't a believer, but he would meet me in the park and sing songs for me. Sometimes he would sing Jewish songs, other times he sang operatic arias. One day he thought he would please me by singing a Christian song, so he sang "Ave Maria." I had to explain that I wasn't that kind of a Christian. I brought him an Intervarsity hymnal and he began singing some of my kind of Christian songs, but since he had never heard them before we had some very unusual renditions.

Afterwards, we'd go out and get some coffee together. He would never come to any of the meetings we conducted at the mission center, but he kept in touch. One day he phoned to let me know he was moving out of town.

"I had to let you know I was leaving," he began. "But I have to know one thing: They would still pay you if you didn't preach there in the park, wouldn't they?"

"Yes, I think so," I said sheepishly. "But what was I going to tell you?"

"It's all right. I liked singing those songs," he replied, chuckling. "And I want to tell you something else. I believe in Jesus."

I never heard from him again.

The other Jewish hecklers continued to engage me, but we had a sort of unwritten code which was impressed upon me because of an incident with a drunk. One of my regular tormentors was shaking a finger in my face, saying, "You traitor! You don't know what you're saying!"

A husky drunk wandered onto the scene and decided to join the attack. He reached up, grabbed my necktie, and was starting to wind up, obviously ready to let me have it. But the old Jewish fellow who had been arguing with me immediately turned on the drunk and shouted, "No, don't, let him alone!"

The drunk was befuddled because he had heard the man berating me. Another heckler ran over and got the park police, and the drunk became even more confused because these were the very people who had been trying to shut me up. Another Jewish onlooker said to the drunk, "You stay out of Jewish business. This is between us Jews."

One thing I have come to appreciate through outdoor preaching is the need to be interesting. If the speaker is dull, the congregation moves on. Another thing is that the speaker must be able to document his statements and avoid exaggeration. The listeners will challenge any statement they consider to be wrong. As I grew more adept in handling these tough outdoor audiences, I realized the most important skill of the successful orator is storytelling, not abstract declamation.

Dealing with hecklers is a colorful, often amusing, and potentially fruitful pursuit for a Jew who follows Jesus. But I've also had to learn how to handle serious theological confrontations. What about the Talmud and the Torah? The law and the prophets? How can a Jewish Christian square his faith in Jesus with Hebrew tradition?

6 LONG LIVE THE LAW
AND THE PROPHETS!

We Jews have always regarded ourselves as a special people. We have suffered and died because we insist on being unique. Our history—the explanation of how and why we became what we are today—is right there in the Torah and the other books of Scripture. But most Jews know little or nothing about any part of the Bible. If my Jewish brethren knew something about their laws and literature, the crazy things I do and say would make more sense to them. I found at the outset of my Los Angeles ministry that when I got into a serious discussion with another Jew, I usually had to make a few points about biblical prophecy. Examining the clear continuities between the Old and New Testaments can be a fascinating experience for Jews who suspect that the hoped-for Messiah may be more than just a fairy tale. And sometimes they even bring the subject up before I do.

Mark, a Jewish Christian in Hollywood, asked me to drop by and talk to a friend of his, and the first thing the fellow said to me was, "I understand you can show me where the Hebrew prophets were referring to Jesus?"

Although I knew that Mark had been doing some preliminary spiritual spadework, I was still somewhat startled by such open interest. But I soon recovered and launched into an explanation of the messianic texts. "Let me show you a verse in Micah 5:2 [5:1 in most Jewish versions]," I said. "You see, it says here that the 'ruler in Israel' will come from Bethlehem. Now who do you know that was born in Bethlehem?"

"David was, wasn't he?"

"Yes. But this was written after David lived and Micah is referring to a future event. Who else?"

"The Christians say Jesus."

"And that's what the New Testament says," I replied, and showed him a relevant passage.

"Now let's turn to Isaiah 53:6," I continued. "As you see, that passage indicates that we're all lost sheep, but it says that God has laid on *him* the iniquity of us all. And further on, in verse 12, Isaiah says 'he hath poured out his soul unto death; and he was numbered

with the transgressors; and he bare the sin of many, and made inter-
cession for the transgressors.' Mark has been telling you something
about his faith and about what the New Testament says. Whom do
you think these two verses refer to?"

"Well, they seem to refer to Jesus."

"Do you know anyone else in history that they could have referred
to?" I pressed.

"No. I suppose not."

"Now I don't want to drown you with verses, but I think you should
read a few more on your own. Here, I'll write them down. There's
Zechariah 9:9, and also Zechariah 12. You should read the entire
passage in Isaiah 53. There are many more, and if you have any
questions, I'll be happy to try to find a verse that will answer them.
You see, I was doing a lot of thinking and wondering about this issue
myself a few years ago. It was my wife who showed me the verses,
and God gave me a conviction they were true. If you ask Him to
give you insight, I know you'll see what I saw and what many other
Jews are seeing these days. These prophecies clearly show that Jesus
is our long-awaited Messiah."

We then said good-bye, and a few days later, in his own time, he
committed his life to Christ. A person has to be ready. You can't
force him before he's prepared to make a genuine commitment.

It would have been impossible to keep score of how many people
I led to Christ, because much of the time the people to whom I had
a ministry accepted Christ privately, outside my presence. I have
always tried to avoid pressuring people. My journals show that in
ten years of ministry in Los Angeles there were 265 Jewish people
who accepted Christ in my presence or shortly after our encounter.
During the same period there were about 1,100 Gentiles who made
a similar commitment.

Some Jews, especially those who have some grounding in the Torah
—the first five books of the Old Testament—or who may be Orthodox in their beliefs, are more receptive to a discussion that centers on
the *Halakah,* or Jewish law, rather than on prophecy. One Orthodox
Jew named Samuel, whom I met through some friends in Los Angeles,
said, "The *Halakah* represents the Word of God to the Jewish people,
and He means for us to follow it. It's only through observance of the
law that a Jew can be justified and holy in God's sight. That's the
reason I observe all the laws in the Torah."

"Good. I only wish I observed all the laws myself," I replied.

He looked a little disconcerted because he knew I was a Christian as well as a Jew. "Why do you want to observe the law? You've rejected it, haven't you?"

"No, I haven't rejected it. Jesus said He came not to destroy but to fulfill the Torah. I know God is pleased when a Jew observes all the law, but I've never met a person who could do it. Tell me, do you ever work on the Sabbath or fail to observe it?"

"Never."

"Well, you're one of the very few people who does that," I replied. "You know, there's an interesting thing that's part of the Sabbath observance. For those Jews who violate the Sabbath, there's a penalty."

"Yes, I know," he said.

"What is it?"

"It's death, according to the Torah."

"Well, tell me, if some other Jew violates the Sabbath, do you keep that part of the law that tells you to carry out the penalty?"

He smiled. "Well, I've never killed a man for not observing it, if that's what you mean."

"That's exactly what I mean. That's part of the law, and you say you observe all the law."

"Well, I observe all of the law that contemporary Orthodox Jews observe. Some parts of the law we can't observe. What if I took it upon myself to kill Jewish homosexuals or those who have committed adultery? The ancient Jewish law may provide for such punishments, but I'd be arrested by the police."

"The only point I'm making is that you don't observe *all* the laws that God handed down to our people, isn't that right?" I responded.

"Technically, you're right."

"But God said—for example, in Leviticus 19:37—that we should keep all of them, didn't He?"

"That He did."

"So where does that leave you?" I asked.

He frowned and said, "A better question might be where does it leave you? You say you're Jewish and you're making an argument for the necessity of observing all the Jewish law. Yet you admit you don't observe most of it. I make an effort at least, but you don't seem to be trying very hard yourself. Nobody's perfect. I don't think God expects that."

"But He does," I replied. "He'll only accept perfect compliance, and if a Jew fails in any small way to keep the law, he's a complete failure in God's eyes. And of course, even the holiest of us do fail.

We've all sinned under the law. So what happens to us? I believe God has provided a way out, a perfect way. That's Jesus, the prom· ised Messiah, the perfect One who died for our sins. If we trust in Him, we can become perfect in God's eyes. Jesus, in other words, can make us kosher."

Samuel disagreed with me, but the seeds of salvation had at least been planted. He had thought himself a good person, near perfect, before our conversation, but I think he had reason afterwards to be less certain of his own righteousness. An awareness of sin, of the impossibility of being in perfect harmony with God through our own efforts, is the first step to understanding the significance of Christ's sacrifice on the cross.

I had a similar discussion with a Conservative Jew named Jake. He regarded the Torah rather literally as the divine Word of God, but he found it more comfortable to interpret the messianic prophecies of the Bible in a symbolic, nonliteral fashion.

"Sure, I'm not perfect, because I don't follow all the old Hebrew laws," he said after I made my point that God expected rigid compliance with the *Halakah*. "But it's a pretty big jump from that point to the idea that Jesus was the culmination of all the prophecies. I think it's a little simplistic to think of the Messiah as a person. 'Messiah' seems to me to refer to a future age or time in which a condition of peace will prevail."

"But most of the messianic passages refer to a person, an individual."

"Those are probably symbolic," he replied.

"By what authority do you say they're symbolic?"

"Well, that's what my rabbi says," he answered.

"Well, God bless your rabbi, but that's a little too convenient. There have been many false messiahs, and he must have gotten tired of waiting. That view may reflect a contemporary version of Judaism, but it's not biblical Judaism. It isn't even consistent with the prayer book I'll bet your rabbi uses."

"I just happen to have a copy of our prayer book here in my home library," he said with a sarcastic edge to his voice. "I'll get it for you and you can show me the inconsistencies."

He was gone for a few seconds and returned with a traditional prayer book that many Conservative and Orthodox synagogues use, called *Daily Prayers,* translated by Dr. A. Th. Philips. He seemed so certain I didn't know what I was talking about that I was beginning to get an almost perverse sort of satisfaction out of the turn the conversation had taken. I took the book from him and began to flip through it until I found several relevant passages. "Many of the Christian doctrines are in this prayer book, but most Jews don't know it," I said. "I didn't know before I accepted Christ. I spent years sitting in synagogue services not really listening to the passages that were being read, or if I did listen, I didn't understand. The fact that the liturgies are read in Hebrew makes it even tougher."

"Okay, less introduction and more solid evidence," Jake said impatiently.

"The New Testament faith is based on the grace of God to give salvation, not on an individual's good works," I said. "Here in the prayer book you have the same concept: 'Not because of our righteous acts do we lay our supplications before Thee, but because of Thine abundant mercies. What is our life? What is our piety? What our righteousness?' Yet Jews often overlook this doctrine and stress only the importance of good works and striving to obey the law. And of course they always fail."

"Okay, but what about the Messiah?"

"There's a prayer for the return of the Messiah right here," I replied. "It says, '. . . to Jerusalem, thy city, return in mercy, and dwell therein as thou hast spoken; rebuild it soon in our days as an everlasting building, and speedily set up therein the throne of David . . . . Speedily cause the offspring of David, thy servant, to flourish, and let his horn be exalted by thy salvation, because we wait for thy salvation all the day.' It's interesting, too, that the Hebrew word for 'salvation' also translates 'Jesus.' "

Jake studied the passage himself for a moment and then leaned back in his seat. "I'll have to agree that, taken literally, that does seem to refer to a personal, individual Messiah, a man who will appear as the offspring of David and bring us salvation. But that's just not the way Jews today, except maybe the Orthodox, interpret it."

"I know that," I agreed, "but the point I'm trying to get across is that whether you refer to the biblical prophecies or to this prayer book, you get a different picture of Judaism than you get in your synagogue. What often passes for Judaism today has no more relation to authentic, biblical Judaism than Unitarianism has to New Testament Christianity."

We discussed a few more sections of the prayer book and then I left him to mull over some of the points that had been made. My problem was to get Jews to turn to *real* Judaism, the Judaism of the law and the prophets, so they could appreciate the significance of

Christ. In their effort to ignore or reject Jesus, many Jews have twisted their own religious traditions beyond recognition. As a matter of fact, my faith is almost indistinguishable from Orthodox Judaism, except for my belief in the grace of God in Christ. Even God's grace, as I pointed out to Jake, is clearly anticipated in the prayer book. But the hope of grace and the promise of salvation are nonexistent in much of contemporary Judaism. The Reform Jews, for example, have another version of the prayer book in which they have deleted all references to the personal Messiah and the rebuilding of the temple. Because of such distortions of Jewish religious tradition, one of my goals has been to get Jews to return to the Judaism of their grandfathers. I know from experience that a Bible-oriented faith can be a natural springboard to a belief in Christ.

Since many Jews aren't particularly interested in Jewish religious traditions, I've also had to learn to answer some distinctively Jewish moral arguments that don't depend directly on religious doctrine. One young man named Larry, who identified himself as an agnostic during a conversation in Los Angeles, said, "I can't believe in a God who would allow six million Jews to be slaughtered by Hitler. A God like that can't possibly be loving. He must be either completely callous or evil if He exists at all."

"But you're concocting your own very narrow conception of what God must be like," I replied. "You're saying that if God exists, He must exist within the framework you yourself have established. If you think about it, you should realize an infinite, all-powerful God can't be bound by the definitions of a finite being like man."

"So what are you saying?" Larry asked. "That God *is* callous or evil? And if He wants to be that way, I shouldn't complain about it?"

"Not at all. God is a loving God, and it pains Him that so many of His chosen people have been killed and persecuted over the years."

"Then why did He let it happen? Why didn't He stop it?"

"I don't pretend to have all the answers," I replied. "But let me tell you what I think about this kind of human suffering. Man was given the capacity to love God and to be given love in return. But for there to be true, genuine love, there has to be a choice. If I can't say, 'No, I don't want to love you,' then it won't be very satisfying for the one receiving my love. I'd be forced to show affection and concern—in effect, be a loving robot."

"That's good theory, good moral philosophy, but how about the dead Jews?" Larry declared.

"Okay, God created man with the power to choose love, peace, humility, and righteousness, but man has instead chosen hatred, war, and pride. The hatred and viciousness came out horribly during the Nazi reign of terror, and God was supremely unhappy and mournful. But He will never violate our right to decide how we deal with one another."

"But the Jews had no choice!" Larry protested. "They've been victims century after century."

"But Jews are no more moral and loving than other men," I replied. "We human beings have collectively chosen to live in a selfish, greedy kind of world. We may sound very righteous when we condemn the gas chambers, but how many of us Jews are prejudiced against black people or other ethnic groups? How many of us boast of our intellect or tarnish the reputations of our neighbors with gossip? We're no more corrupt than other people, but we're certainly no less corrupt either.

"It was a series of historical decisions that permitted the Third Reich to grow and prosper—decisions by ordinary human beings, like you and me. We play dumb and look the other way. We look upon the misery of fellow human beings as somebody else's business, but not our own. Like Cain, we shrug and say, 'Am I my brother's keeper?' Each of us has responded to the privilege of decision-making with a lifetime of irresponsible choices. And you ask, 'Where was God?' I'll tell you where He was. He was watching us, all of us, and He was weeping."

Larry thought for a moment and then asked, "So do you see any significance at all to the fact that six million Jews were killed?"

"Sure," I replied, "but what I focus on is the fact that twelve million of us were preserved alive. If Haman in Esther's time and the Pharaoh of the Exodus and Hitler had achieved their goals, none of us would be alive. Anti-Semitism hasn't come into existence since the time of Christ. Jews have always been oppressed and hated. Don't look at the hole, look at the doughnut. The survival of the Jewish people, if you look at world history, can only be explained by supernatural intervention. We've outlasted our oppressors not because we were great militarists or because we isolated ourselves from all other peoples in some remote corner of the world or because our religious convictions are so strong. And it's not because we were smarter, because often we weren't. There is no natural cause or course of action that we took that could account for our survival. There has to be another explanation, and I think it's that God has a reason for our survival and He has preserved the Jewish people the way He preserved Job."

"But what about the future?" he asked. "I think it's a cop out to say we don't have to do anything for ourselves because God will take care of us. Don't you think we should prepare to defend ourselves? Don't you think it would have been better during World War II if all the Jews had risen up and fought Hitler?"

"You're focusing on the fact that Hitler killed the Jews, and I've already told you I don't do that," I said. "Some Jews are so frightened and angry and resentful about Hitler that they can't think of anything else. They show pictures of bodies piled up from the concentration camps. But what these people forget is that Jews haven't survived because of force. What could the small minority of Jews have done against Hitler? And it wasn't just Hitler. It was the hateful climate that allowed him to exist."

Such encounters gave me experience in explaining my Christian faith in a Jewish context, but in one sense I may have become too competent for my own good during this ministry in Los Angeles. Dr. Fuchs at the American Board of Missions to the Jews in New York asked me to organize a training program for candidates in Jewish missionary work. In 1965 I was made director of recruiting and training, and the Mission's board of directors voted to transfer the entire program to New York City. I finally moved in 1967 and on my arrival was given the position of missionary in charge of Headquarters District. By then, I was well on my way toward becoming a religious organization man.

The admissions' procedure for the training program we instituted was not easy. The candidate's college and seminary transcripts were carefully evaluated, he was given a battery of personality tests which were interpreted to us by a psychologist, and he had to complete nine employment forms, including a fourteen-page doctrinal questionnaire.

Upon induction the candidate was told he would be expected to be on duty or in training from eight in the morning to ten in the evening, six days a week for six months. The classes of candidates were small—only four to six students. They began their training in dungarees. If a person wasn't willing to wash windows, sweep the sidewalk, or mop floors, he would never become a missionary to the Jews through our program.

Lectures were held four times a day and on the following day examinations were given on the material covered in each of the previous sessions. They learned Hebrew one hour every day, but the majority of the lectures, most of which I delivered, dealt with the simple "how to" subjects of missionary work. Each of the candidates was also assigned to work for four hours with experienced missionaries who reflected the whole gamut of evangelistic experience.

As the training program and other mission activities mushroomed, I became more and more entangled in organizational commitments. I preached to the congregation each Sunday at the Beth Sar Shalom Center, taught two Bible classes every week, and managed to give additional sermons at two or three churches each week. There were numerous committee meetings to discuss our own missionary strategy, and I was an active member on the committees or boards of several other evangelistic agencies. I also headed a building program established to remodel our headquarters facility at a cost of $168,000. My responsibilities included designing the chapel, kitchen, and fellowship hall. In addition to juggling all these jobs, I had to supervise the work and training of fourteen to eighteen people on my mission staff.

I continued to preach on street corners once a week, but slowly I began to insulate myself from evangelistic personal encounters. I was doing too much talking and not enough listening. The results were almost disastrous.

7 THE GREENING OF A HIPPIE HATER

The hippie movement, antiwar protests, and general disenchantment of young people with the establishment were gaining momentum before I reached New York City. But, virtually oblivious to the social storm that was swirling about in the streets, I shut my office door and settled snugly into my new administrative role. The American Board of Missions to the Jews would have been flexible enough to let me examine more closely this youthful revolution, but frankly, I had no desire to get involved.

Although I had been a free-wheeling, creative evangelist in Los Angeles, I lost some verve in the transition to leadership in New York. I gradually became a self-satisfied religious bureaucrat who was more concerned with running an efficient organization than with showing compassion to other human beings.

My uniform at work was similar to that of almost any other straight businessman: dark suit, thin tie, clean-shaven face, even a crew cut. And my negative views on youthful radicals and antiestablishment demonstrations coincided with my conservative dress. I didn't give much thought to being a real person to other people. I didn't think I had time for that sort of thing. Being warm and compassionate evangelists was the job of the missionaries who worked under me. I became more and more ensconced in a highly structured environment, where people could be treated like cases. Nobody could tell me anything about being a human being, because I knew it all. After all, Dr. Fuchs and the other top people at the American Board had thought enough of me to promote me, hadn't they?

My job now was to dispense my vast knowledge to those under me, and it took a bit of conscious humility on my part to listen to their suggestions at all.

Although I was rather satisfied with my administrative role, I began to feel a general discomfort from an entirely different and unexpected direction: my own identity as a Jew. I had been a Jew all my life and had lived in Jewish communities and participated in the Jewish religious traditions. Even while I was in California, I had expanded my knowledge of what it meant to be a Jew and how to communicate to Jews the meaning of my faith in Jesus. But in the late 1960s in New York, I discovered that a change had occurred in my Jewishness. My own identity as a Jew was subtly slipping away.

The churches where I spoke recognized me as a Jew, a Hebrew Christian, but I wasn't doing anything to be a Jew. God's stamp on me as one of His chosen people seemed elusive, almost unimportant. I read Jewish journals, but I didn't feel any commitment to the Jewish people other than a desire to witness about Christ. I felt uncomfortable in synagogue, because I always suspected that if the rabbi knew who I was he wouldn't want me there. In short, I had become what you might call a Gentile's Jew. My values had become white Anglo-Saxon Protestant rather than those of a Jew who had accepted Jesus. A thought kept nagging deep inside me that as a Jew I had to be less WASPish and more Jewish, regardless of what other Jews or Christians thought of me. But my vague, undefined sense of dissatisfaction was not enough to make me change my life. God had to hit me over the head a couple of times to get me back on the track.

One bombshell was my mother's death. She had never approved of my Christian commitment and rarely pulled any punches in conveying her disappointment. One day when we were riding past a Denver church in which I was scheduled to speak, I pointed out my name, posted in large letters on the bulletin board. She shook her head and said, "It's like you stuck a knife through my heart."

But despite our religious differences, we always loved each other and shared our common heritage with great relish. When she passed away, I felt that a part of me, a part of my own culture and history, had gone with her. I also realized I had been failing to develop my own personal identity as a Jew. I had been relying too much on memories of the past rather than continuing my family's vital Jewish traditions in my daily life.

I resolved to do something about it, but what? I looked around and prayed in an effort to find an answer, and God soon showed me the way. The occasion was a speech I gave at an Intervarsity Christian Fellowship meeting at Columbia University. My topic was "Hippies, Radicals, and Revolutionaries," and my approach was to make fun of them. As a rather narrow-minded organization man, I had little patience with anyone who rejected the old American work ethic and ran off into the hills to contemplate the flowers and the sky and strum a guitar all day long. I got a laugh at one point when I quoted Ronald Reagan's quip, "A hippie is someone who dresses like Tarzan, walks like Jane, smells like Cheetah, says, 'Make love, not war,' but is incapable of doing either."

After the meeting was over, I thought I had made a rather good impression and was feeling satisfied with my presentation. But a friend of mine, Bob Berk, a Hebrew-Christian social worker, walked over and asked with a serious expression, "Did you ever smell a hippie?"

Thinking he was kidding, I replied, "No, I never got close enough."

But I quickly saw he was not only serious but a little angry. "What you're doing is alienating a lot of the people you should be trying to reach," he declared. "Do you know that a lot of hippies are Jewish? Do you know what they're saying, how they feel? What are you doing to try to talk to these people?"

I was crestfallen and defensive because he was attacking me like this, and I returned his anger with a little of my own. "I don't want to talk to people who don't want to talk to me."

I changed the subject as soon as possible, but his criticism bothered me all that evening and into the next day after I had arrived at work. I looked around me and didn't like what I saw. Even if those hippies had wanted to talk to me, they wouldn't have had a chance. I was very difficult to approach. You had to go through a receptionist, then a secretary, and finally into a waiting room where an assistant minister would chat with you for a while. Most people who walked in off the street never saw me, unless they made an appointment well in advance. I simply wasn't available. Jesus had commanded, "Go ye therefore . . ." (Matthew 22:9), but I was in effect saying, "Come here to me and if you're lucky . . . ."

My first step was to seek help from a young woman named Susan Alexander who, I knew, was familiar with the youthful counterculture.

"Why don't you get out and talk to some of these kids?" Susan suggested. "You stay couped up here in this office too much."

"Where should I go?" I asked. "What should I do?"

"Go down to Greenwich Village and sit around. You'll find hippies are easy enough to talk to."

Following her suggestion, I set Wednesdays aside for my own education. I read in the morning and went out on the streets in the afternoon. Manhattan's Washington Square Park in the heart of the Village was my outdoor classroom. I just sat around on the park benches and listened to the shaggy, blue-jean-clad young people as they rapped with each other. In some cases, they were saying what Christians had been saying for centuries: "Love is *it,* man. That's where it's at." They were concerned with experiencing life. They weren't concerned with abstractions. Ideas were important but only as they led to personal relationships.

I occasionally walked over to a group and said, "Hi, what's going on?" Sometimes, I'd get into a chess game, and although I'm prob-

ably the world's worst chess player, the competition provided opportunities for discussion. As Susan had predicted, I found it easy and
pleasant to talk with them. Back in my ivory-towered office I had
been disdainful toward hippies because I was ignorant, totally un-
familiar with their hang-loose life-style.

After listening for a few days, I knew I wanted to say something
of substance to these people, but I didn't know how to go about it.
We had mountains of standard gospel literature, but none of it seemed
appropriate. The language and the concepts were off target. They
seemed too preachy and humorless. I told Bob Berk about my problem one day, and he said, "Don't be lazy, Moishe. You should write
your own stuff. Tailor it to these people and the way they think. You
can't be some kind of distant intellectual. That approach to Jewish
hippies—any hippies, for that matter—is all wrong. You have to show
them you really care."

I scrawled out a simple homemade tract in my own hand on a
single sheet of paper and experimented until I found an effective way
to fold it. The title was "A Message From Squares," and I drew a
simple, obese figure of myself on the front. The hip jargon is dated
now, but I found it got the message across:

Hey, you with the beard!
We think you are Beautiful.
God likes long hair and beards, too.
He didn't want the Israelites to trim their beards.
Can you just imagine Moses or Elijah with a crew cut?
You are brave to do your own thing.
Most of us don't have the heart to make the scene.

. . . We both want LOVE but we settle for either sex or sermons.
All want Life. Most get a kind of living death called existence.

We try to be the saviours of the world, and we just end up sinning
   against those we want to save.
Maybe Jesus, the real Saviour, can save us, give us peace and help
   us come alive, to live and love. . . .

Then I quoted John 3:16.
I signed my name and put my office address underneath. Although
this little composition was not the greatest work of literature, I felt
every word of it. I had no way of knowing this tract would be a fore-
runner of the later Jews-for-Jesus "broadsides," which we've distributed in the millions. I just wanted to communicate to these young

people, and many of them sensed my genuine concern. I identified myself with the establishment, but I let them know I wanted to listen to
them, too. Handing out a few of these around the Village helped
start some conversations I'd never have dreamed possible a month
before: "Hey, man, this is way out!" I essentially have a middle-class
outlook on life, but I've always believed in a revolutionary Christianity. And that belief was now motivating me to crack the stagnant
mold I had constructed for myself. I began to keep my office door
open, and I told our receptionist to send up any hippies who wandered
in off the street.

A major change was occurring in my approach to people: One
year before, if a bearded kid wearing sandals had asked for me, he'd
never have made it through the first layer of defenses I had set up to
protect myself. Now, there was a steady stream of street people going
in and out of my office. Some days, I'd end up with wall-to-wall hippies. They'd walk up to the receptionist and ask, "Hey, man, does
Moishe Rosen live here?" and she would send them up.

There were two young girls in particular, Enid and Rita, who kept
coming back, and I learned a lot from them. They lived in a commune which they said was an attempt to reproduce the life-style of a
recent science-fiction novel called *Stranger in a Strange Land* by
Robert A. Heinlein. They were standard street kids, sexually quite
frank and free. They asked me a lot of questions, especially about
Jesus.

"Was there any religion around your home?" I asked Enid one day.

"Oh, my mother and father are Jewish, but I'm not," she replied.
"I don't have any religion."

"So what do you think about religion in general?" I asked.

"All religion is groovy, but you guys mess it up by saying Jesus
is the only way," she said. "What beautiful thing ever happened because of Jesus? Did anybody plant flowers anyplace because of Him?
You save souls, but people die of hunger."

They expressed social concerns which I had been ignoring, and so
my answers were rather inadequate, I'm afraid. But ecology became
an issue for me, and so did the question of social action as a means
to make the world a better place.

"Your slogan is 'Kill a Commie for Christ,' isn't it?" Enid asked
on one occasion, and that shook me up. I knew devout Christians
who weren't far from that attitude, so closely did they link God and
country.

Most hippies I met were basically sweet, sensitive, concerned people. Rita had adopted her own little old lady on the upper West Side, and she made regular visits to cheer up the woman, do errands, make her life a little more beautiful. I knew that inwardly, Jesus made my life beautiful, but Rita was a good lesson for me because I could see my own deficiencies in showing compassion to others.

The personal morals of many of these kids were nothing to brag about, but they were perceptive. They asked good questions. From their questions there eventually came some satisfactory answers which other Jews for Jesus and I have translated into illustrated tracts.

My life, then, was changing, or "greening" as author Charles Reich might say. I was getting involved in Jewish matters again, but this time my perspective was that of the young Jews from the so-called counter-culture. Because I was praying, asking God for guidance, trying to keep myself open to His leading, I felt I was moving in the right direction. But I wanted to be sure, so I asked Dr. Fuchs if I could go on a speaking tour of seminaries for the purpose of recruiting new candidates in San Francisco, the heart of the hippie phenomenon. I thought that by going out there and observing the social revolution firsthand, I'd be in a better position to know the direction that God wanted me to take. Dr. Fuchs agreed, and early in 1970 I flew to the West Coast to give addresses at Simpson College, Conservative Baptist Theological Seminary, and Golden Gate Baptist Seminary.

Between lectures, I visited several Christian communes, walked around on the streets of San Francisco, and watched the youth culture in action. At one Bible study I attended, which was conducted by evangelist Jack Sparks, hippies were sitting outside the windows and doors in an effort to hear the teaching of God's Word. They were spiritually hungry and so full of energy and zeal. We had a "right-on" group of young people in New York, but nothing could compare with the radiance of the people I saw out there.

Still, I was afraid my positive reaction to the San Francisco hippie scene might be predominantly my own feeling, and not very practical or the result of God's leading. And so I went off by myself one morning into some hills north of the city. It was foggy and dreary, a reflection of the troubled and uncertain way I felt about my own future. I reached a grape arbor at the top of the hill and said, "Lord, I really wish I were back here in California. Show me what to do." The fog lifted just after I reached the arbor, and I could see below me that the city was just emerging from the fog. The sunlight came through, shining on the underside of the clouds and reflecting downward so that, in the early morning light, the city was made gold. I sensed a feeling of reassurance, a feeling that the things I wanted would come to pass. I knew somehow that it wasn't wrong for me to return to California.

When I arrived back in New York, I still didn't know precisely what God had in store, but I felt strongly that California was where I had to go. When I told Dr. Fuchs about my desire to go to the West Coast and work with students and street people, he was justifiably skeptical. I wasn't exactly anyone's ideal image of the youth worker, because I weighed an all-time high of 327 pounds, was still an extremely conservative dresser, and had my crew cut shorn even shorter than usual. But that wasn't all. I was thirty-eight years old and had no special experience or training in youth work. My best experience was that I was father to a daughter as old as most of these kids, but her own life had been so different from theirs. She had been a Christian since she was sixteen and a Sunday school teacher. However, I could talk to her and she understood what I was saying. Maybe they would understand, too.

Although Dr. Fuchs had trusted my judgment in the past, I could understand why he had some questions about this request, which seemed crazy on its face. But he has always been a forward-looking administrator, ready to try new things if he thinks there's any chance they may further God's work. So he allowed me to resign my double role as missionary in charge and as director of recruiting and gave me two of the mission's cars. In the summer of 1970, accompanied by eight females—my wife, two daughters, and five other girls who had either worked for the American Board or held other jobs in New York—I headed west. Even the family dog came along. I had a general idea that I wanted to continue to spread the gospel to Jews and also that I wanted to get involved with the youth culture. Beyond that, I didn't know what I was doing. I suspected that some of the evangelism techniques I had developed would be applicable to my new ministry, but I was also certain that I'd have a lot of learning to do.

We spent our first months in San Francisco finding places to live and getting our feet on the ground. Corte Madera, California, just north of San Francisco, became our headquarters, and from there we ranged over the entire Bay area. When we started mixing with the young street people, I realized the dark suits and skinny ties had to go. Wearing blue jeans, we passed out tracts and rapped with anyone who would listen on the streets and campuses. Soon after I arrived, an incident with a couple of young female hitchhikers impressed on me that my old staid ways were gone forever.

As a general rule, I never picked up hitchhikers in New York, and even in California I tell our girls that they're foolish to stop for anyone. But I've found that, for myself, stopping for people can provide an opportunity to rap about Jesus. So it was natural, as I was returning from the airport one day, to pull over to the side of the road and pick up two girls who had their thumbs out. They got settled in the car and we talked amiably for a few moments. Then, almost without warning, one of them said, "Do you want to make love to us?"

I was flabbergasted, but I managed a slight smile. A year earlier, I might have thought, "How dare you, you little tart? Don't you realize I'm a Christian, and a very important one at that?" But I now knew too much about the counterculture to give that kind of response.

"Well, you're very pretty girls, and I appreciate your offer," I said. "But I've got this idea that God is always watching me. But the fact that you wanted to do something for me makes me feel better."

One smiled. "We just wanted to cheer you up," she said. "How come you look so sad?"

"Well, I'm a little tired now, and when I relax completely, my face sets into a frown. But actually I'm not really sad. I'm really quite happy because I've found a way of life that satisfies me very much."

We continued to chat about our respective attitudes toward life and God, and I finally dropped them off at an intersection. They were thoughtful girls but they made no pretense about affirming a Christian morality. They had no sense of shame or sin, and I couldn't expect them to measure their lives by my Christian standards. All I could do was plant a few ideas about Jesus. Their offer of sex was an attempt to show kindness, and I had learned enough about hippies to take it that way and continue to communicate. As I drove toward Corte Madera, I knew things were going well. I had really arrived where I was supposed to be—California, the heart of the counterculture, the center of the work God had given me as a Jew for Jesus.

8 MEANWHILE, BACK AT THE RANCH

While I was getting initiated into the hippie scene in San Francisco, some unusual things were happening in the backwoods of Oregon that would have a tremendous impact on my ministry. A middle-aged Christian, Jack Dunn, and his wife, Liz, felt called by God to prepare their house. Jack said God told him that He was going to send some people to them and that the couple should feed and love these visitors.

Although Jack explained that God spoke to him directly through a voice and a vision, the exact purpose of his task was not revealed. But he and Liz obeyed by immediately furnishing and repairing their extra rooms. One of the first groups to arrive after the preparations were completed were some motorcycle roughnecks. One of the Dunns' later guests, Mark Winter, called these people "bikers, heavy-duty greasers." They put Jack and Liz through a lot of grief. They ruined part of a field Jack had planted and they got stoned on pills and dope. Jack finally put his foot down. He said that nobody who stayed there could possess or use any drugs.

Needless to say, the Christian couple seemed baffled as to why God wanted them to take care of these Hell's Angels types, especially since the bikers didn't seem particularly interested in the gospel. But soon, this bunch moved on, and a different breed of guest started wandering in. These were all hippies, and most of them were Jewish. Jack's house, which has become known affectionately as "the ranch," eventually became a quiet stopping place for scores of young Jews, a retreat with an atmosphere that encouraged serious consideration of the claims of Jesus Christ.

One of the early Jewish visitors up there was Baruch Goldstein, a stocky, bearded young man from the Bronx who eventually joined me in San Francisco. Baruch, who laughs and jokes as much as anyone I know, had led a wild, adventurous life before wandering into the Oregon haven. He was a typical hippie with the "turn on, tune in, drop out" philosophy. Knowing he would confront the inevitable draft, he joined the army. He served as a combat soldier in Vietnam, was wounded and began receiving a disability pension on his discharge. Just before he was released from the service, he got involved in drugs in a naval hospital in New York. That experience encouraged him to buy a small bus with his steady veteran's pension and head toward a life of drugs and sex in the counterculture.

"I tried heroin, a lot of grass, and I'd sell anything," he explained. "I moved out to California and lived in a couple of communes, traveled around, did anything I wanted. Girls, dope, I enjoyed it all. But then I heard that my brother, Fred, had become a Christian and that he was staying in Oregon at a place called 'the ranch.' I really couldn't believe it. I always thought people who believed in Jesus were weak, so I decided I had to talk to him about it.

"I stopped off in a forest on the way up to the ranch to have some lunch and smoke some dope. But all of a sudden this car came up and a guy jumped out. He handed me a piece of paper and drove off without a word. I glanced at the paper and saw that his testimony was written on it: 'I used to be a dope-smoking, pill-popping hippie until Jesus came into my life and set me free.'

"I thought 'Wow! I must be getting into Jesus country.'

"When I arrived in the town that was closest to the ranch, I knew I was in trouble. For all practical purposes, the ranch was inaccessible. There were only two ways to get out there: You either hiked about forty miles through the woods and came in from behind, or you had to find a boat that was hidden in some bushes outside the town and then row across this huge river. Daniel Boone couldn't have located the place even if he had radar. I had been told to call Jack at the ranch and then either get him or someone else to come over and meet me. I didn't have his phone number, so I decided to turn left and call the town operator from a small drugstore. But I couldn't turn left because of a couple of cars coming from the opposite direction, so I turned right into a gas station. The operator told me Jack had an unlisted number, and none of the old New York tricks I had up my sleeve would work it out of her. I said it was an emergency, I had to speak to my brother, but nothing moved her."

Baruch was thoroughly frustrated at this point. "I was tired, hungry, and cold, but then I came up with an idea. It was a small town, only a few thousand people. I decided if I started asking enough people, somebody was bound to know Jack. So I walked up to this man, a weird-looking guy with a gray beard, who was getting gasoline for his bus. I said, 'Excuse me, do you know a Jack Dunn?'

" 'What do you want to find that kook for?' he said.

"I was happy and upset at the same time—upset that this guy seemed so uptight, but happy that the first person I met knew Jack. The guy said, 'Wait right here,' and he went to the gas-station phone. A few minutes later, he motioned me over and handed me the receiver. My brother Freddy was on the other end of the line! But that was only half the surprise. The guy I'd been talking to, the first person I walked up to in the town—and at a gas station I hadn't even wanted to turn into—was Jack Dunn himself! 'Wow, what a coincidence!' I said. 'Coincidence, ha!' Jack knowingly replied."

Baruch recalled that after he'd been at the ranch for a few days, he felt there was something different about the place. "I really sensed a different kind of love there, and that made me question a lot of things. One of the other hippies suggested that I start reading the New Testament to find the answers to what I was looking for. I got zapped out by the Holy Spirit somewhere between Matthew and Revelation. The Sermon on the Mount really made an impression. I could see the adulterous, sinful, lustful life I had been living."

In an effort to find an answer, Baruch said, "I began to pray, at first like the scribes and Pharisees. I asked for a sign or a miracle because I decided I wasn't a fool, I wasn't going to believe in nothing. 'Dear God,' I said, 'please split a river for me or send down a thunderbolt.' Well, God showed the miraculous to me, but it wasn't what I thought it would be. It was a very simple, subtle thing. I saw the miracle one morning when I awoke and watched the others getting together for breakfast and praying. It was us, you and me, His creation. I knew inside of me that there was a God, but I still didn't understand Jesus. Then I continued to read the New Testament, and God showed me Jesus was the Promised One, the Messiah of the Old Testament. I fell for it hook, line, and sinker. God went fishing, and I got caught."

Baruch's life underwent an immediate, radical change. "I completely gave up drugs. Before I became a Christian, I sold anything anybody would buy. I used to fly from California to New York with a cargo of grass. In New York, I'd pick up some heroin and bring it back to California. But after I discovered Jesus, my cargo changed. Now, when I fly, I take thousands of gospel tracts east, distribute them, and return with a tremendous sense of accomplishment and satisfaction that drugs could never give me."

His faith in Christ also encouraged him to rediscover his identity as a Jew. "When I was into the hippie scene, I remember writing a letter home saying, 'Dear Brother and Sister' instead of 'Dear Mom and Dad.' I wanted to tear down all ethnic and social walls and traditions. I considered myself to be Baruch from the universe, rather than Baruch the Jew. But I started seeing the significance of my Jewish heritage at the ranch. We conducted a Sabbath service while I stayed there, and since then I've started going to synagogue fairly

regularly. I believe God created the situation at the ranch so that
young Jews could find Christ. The large majority of hippies who
visited there were Jewish, and many of them have contributed to the
work of the Jews for Jesus. The ranch doesn't exist anymore—it was
flooded after about a year—and Jack and Liz have moved on to another town. But as short-lived as their ranch experience was, they
were there when God needed them. Their work at the ranch occurred
almost simultaneously with the beginning of Moishe's San Francisco
ministry. Some might say the timing was just a coincidence, but I've
seen too many such 'coincidences' to believe God didn't have a hand
in it."

Another one of the ranch crowd and a close friend of Baruch's
from New York, Jh'an Moskowitz, had an even more startling encounter with God.

"I come from a Conservative Jewish family," explained Jh'an, a
lanky, bearded fellow who would rather argue a philosophical issue
than eat. "My father and mother were in a Nazi concentration camp,
and my dad still has the number stamped on his arm. My people had
suffered because of their Jewishness, and I knew from an early age
just how serious a thing it was to be a Jew. It was always *them* and
us. Them included the Nazis and Christians."

Jh'an's early commitment to his people culminated when he joined
a Zionist group and volunteered at the age of seventeen for the Israeli
army during the 1967 war against Egypt. "I decided I'd rather die
in Israel than in Vietnam, but I never was officially admitted into a
combat unit. I stayed in the reserves and lived on a kibbutz, but then
I began to realize that war wasn't where it was at for me. Although I
still supported Israel, I saw a subtle racism over there. The Arab refu-
gees were treated pretty poorly, and I didn't like that. So, disillusioned,
I started looking for personal truth in the youth subculture."

He graduated from Long Island University, but the thought of an
ordinary, middle-class career repulsed him. So he retreated into drugs
and sex and finally decided to head out west. "Baruch and I got together out here in California, and we planned to become psychedelic
pirates," Jh'an said. "We met some old friends in the Bay area and
got into dealing and using all kinds of dope. I was really crass toward
girls because I only wanted them as sex objects.

"We were living in San Francisco in a commune called the Freaky
Dude Ranch when a couple of our close friends became Christians. I
had read some of the Bible, but Jesus didn't seem real to me. Things
began to get a little boring and repetitive around the commune—

the same sex, the same drugs, over and over—so I decided to take a vacation in the Caribbean."

Jh'an hitchhiked to Florida and worked in a warehouse for a couple of weeks to earn enough money for the plane fare to Jamaica. "I was still looking for truth, so I headed for the Jamaican hills and sought out some tribesmen I'd heard about who were supposed to worship the Ethiopian emperor, Haile Selassie. I lived in a hut with a guy named Joshua and tried to learn the spiritual truths I thought these people had to offer. One old wise man used to say to me in a deep voice with a rolling Jamaican accent, 'King of kings and Lord of lords, Conquering Lion from the tribe of Judah. Though your skin may be white, if you smoke the herb, the blood in your heart will be black.' So I puffed on his grass and really grooved on everything he said. Many things seem especially profound when you're stoned.

"But I had overstayed my visa, and the authorities came looking for me. I had to hightail it out of there and head back to the States. Still, I was no wiser than I had been a month or a year before. And I got a shock when I received a letter from the commune: Baruch had become a Christian. I really felt bad, like I'd lost a friend. I could see the others getting on the Jesus kick, but not Baruch. He was a stone-cold heathen, a jolly, fun-loving guy who hadn't even been looking for anything. I, at least, had been on a spiritual quest. I thought, that's really heavy, man."

Jh'an returned to San Francisco in April, 1971, and at the request of one of his old hippie buddies, Mitch Glaser, who had recently become a Christian, he attended a Bible study I was teaching in San Francisco. Jh'an's concept of a Christian was simply a person who loved other people. By that definition, he thought he might be a Christian himself. Mitch introduced me to Jh'an and asked me to rap with him about Jesus.

"Do you believe Jesus Christ died for you, Jh'an?" I asked.

"Yeah, man, I go for that," Jh'an replied.

"And do you believe he was resurrected from the dead?"

"Sure."

After a few more such questions, I decided that what Jh'an said he believed was similar to what any Christian would believe. But I didn't know him too well at that time, and he told me later that in retrospect he's convinced he wasn't a Christian at that point.

"No change had come about in my life when I first talked to Moishe," Jh'an explained. "I didn't see why a faith in Christ should affect the way I lived. If someone offered me dope, I took it without really thinking about it. In other words, I hadn't really committed myself. Because I was still looking for spiritual knowledge, I hitchhiked up to the ranch to see what Baruch was doing. It was a heavy experience for me. After staying there three days, I decided I had to get out. Everybody was talking about God this and God that. I tried to inject my own ideas I had just dreamed up about Jesus—the cosmic Jesus. But my intellectualized Christ had no impact on my daily life, no relationship to the personal God these people seemed to know. I wanted to believe, but I couldn't force myself. I asked God to give me a real experience. I had to know that He was really, really who the Bible said He was. I couldn't do it on blind faith. I had to know it was more than a psychological high."

The night before he left the ranch, Jh'an said he had a dream: "Some dark-haired young lady came up behind me and put her arms around my shoulders and began to seduce me. When I woke up, her face was vague in my memory, but I did recall a distinctive way her arms crept around me, and a peculiar kind of dress she was wearing. I thought, 'Tsk, tsk, God, what a horrible dream.' I had some idea it was from God, but I also suspected it might have resulted from some kind of psychological suggestion from the Jesus freaks who were all around me at the ranch. At any rate, I ignored any special religious significance.

"Baruch told me the next morning that he was ready to return to San Francisco, and he asked me if I wanted a lift. I accepted, and on the way down I mentioned my dream in passing and said that it was really far out because I thought God had seduced me. He thought I was goofing on God, that I'd really never had the dream. He accused me of being really gross and didn't talk much more to me during the trip.

"Baruch dropped me off at about midnight at my commune and then drove down the street to see Mitch Glaser at another apartment. When I walked through my front door, I realized all of a sudden what a dark scene I was into. The place looked like Sodom and Gomorrah. All the speed freaks were there and everyone was stoned, tripped out. People had painted their faces and were dancing around like maniacs. Remembering the beautiful, peaceful scene in Oregon, I didn't feel like getting involved with them just then. I decided this wasn't where things were at. These people were really blowing themselves out. I went back to the kitchen and tried to get my head together. But while I was standing with my hands resting on the sink, I felt these arms start to slide over my shoulders. I looked around out of the corner of my eye, and this chill went up my spine. The girl behind me had the same dress pattern, the same general physical features of the chick in my dream at the ranch. I flipped out! The dream was actually coming true. I didn't move. It was really heavy.

"I thought, 'Is this really happening, man? Maybe God's really real. Maybe He's trying to tell me something.' Meanwhile, this chick was really coming on strong. She said, 'What's going on? Let's get it on.' I shrugged and said to myself, 'Look, Jh'an, don't freak her out.' She started running her hands up and down my body, and I got excited and decided God would forgive me this time. So I turned around and put my arms around her and looked over her shoulder. Suddenly, everything went BOING! On the window in front of me, the sign of the cross had been traced clearly in the frost on the glass. As it happened, Baruch and Mitch had been walking outside just at that moment. Mitch, as was his custom, drew that cross on the window, but neither of them could see me through the glass. Coincidences were one thing, but this was too much. There was a pattern now that I couldn't deny, and I knew I wasn't hallucinating on drugs. I hadn't had any dope for several days because it was prohibited at the ranch. I said to myself, 'Hey Jh'an, enough coincidences! Let's get it together and find out what you've got to do.' I met Mitch and Baruch just after they came through the door and said, 'Look, fellows, I think God is real. Maybe I'd better get together with Him, maybe He's really there. Let's go have a talk.' "

As they walked toward a nearby park, Jh'an told Baruch, "Hey, man, the dream really came true. What should I do?"

"Maybe you should ask God to come into your life, give yourself over to Him," Baruch suggested.

"Well, if the Guy's real, why should I run away from Him?"

When they reached the park, Jh'an got down on his knees, and Baruch and Mitch laid their hands on his head. Jh'an prayed, "Father, forgive me for pretending I knew You, for being the imperfect person I am. Come into my life, take it over, I'm Yours."

In explaining his commitment, Jh'an said, "Coincidences that lead to a spiritual commitment don't happen in an isolated way. There may be a couple of minor external events that don't seem too remarkable to an objective observer. But in my case—and I know this is true for other Christians as well—there's a corresponding internal event, an insight God provides that ties the coincidences together and produces a divine revelation. That's what happened to me with that dream incident."

These fellows gravitated in my direction initially because of a strange experience that Mitch Glaser had in Sausalito. He had spent some time at the ranch but was still into the hip scene, unsure of what direction his life should take. While sitting near the shore in Sausalito, he prayed that God would show him what to do, and almost immediately one of my broadsides, bearing my name and address, came floating up in the tide. He hitched over to our house, knocked on the door, and declared, "The Lord sent me to you. What should I do?"

"I don't know," I said, somewhat taken aback. "Don't ask me, ask Him."

"I did, and He sent me here," Mitch replied. "What should I do?"

"I don't know," I answered again. We were at something of an impasse, but I wouldn't attempt to tell him something I didn't know myself. That's one thing I won't budge on: I know an individual should accept Jesus as Lord, love God, read the Bible, lead a Christian life, and pray. But as for the specific direction of life's affairs, he'll have to go to God himself to find the answer. We talked for a while longer, and he rode with me to a nearby shop to get some bagels and then headed back toward the ranch. While he was up there, Mitch asked Jack Dunn if he knew me. Jack replied that he didn't, but that God had told him I was okay. The next time I got together with Mitch, he had Baruch and Jh'an in tow, and they were all Christians.

"I'm hungry," I said when I joined them on that occasion. "Why don't we go have some Chinese food?"

They accepted my invitation, and we headed toward an inexpensive Chinatown restaurant. We each ordered huge amounts of food, but when the check came, I found I had left my wallet at home. Baruch had to dig into his pockets and pay with some of his army disability money. I learned later that Baruch was a little disconcerted with me at that point: "I wondered what kind of guy this was," he said. "He asks you out to eat and then you have to pay for it."

But he soon forgot about the meal after we walked outside the restaurant. I began to show them how I conducted my street ministry by pulling out five hundred or so broadsides and handing them out to pedestrians. Baruch was so fascinated that he grabbed them away from me and started distributing them himself. He was like a child and kept saying, "Look, people really take them! Look at that guy— he's walking down the street reading it! Hey, man, this is really terrific!"

"I really liked handing out those tracts," Baruch recalled. "It was flipping me out that I was standing there on a street corner in downtown San Francisco dealing out gospel literature. I always had this stereotype of Jesus freaks walking around with their placards warning. 'Repent! The World Is Doomed!' And there I was doing essentially the same thing myself—and enjoying it."

While Baruch was getting high handing out the pamphlets, Mitch was just staring at him in utter fascination. And Jh'an, who will argue about any subject under the sun, whether he knows anything about it or not, was interrogating me on some esoteric theological point. It was almost surrealistic. But as weird as that tableau must have seemed to any onlookers, I realize now it marked the beginning of some friendships that were to be significant for evangelism among the Jews in the Bay area. The Jews for Jesus were gradually drifting together, feeling their way into a working relationship.

But before I leave the ranch episode, I want to mention something about Mark Winter, another graduate of Jack Dunn's Oregon hide-away. He's an aggressive tract passer and is becoming involved in helping us in film work and photography, his specialty during graduate school. But the Mark Winter of today and the Mark of the ranch are two different people, for he suffered from a severe case of "ranchitis."

Ranchitis was a spiritual malady characterized by enjoying Jesus into a state of almost total inactivity. Some would describe it as an immersion in mysticism, and others would call it grooving on Jesus.

Mark explained his condition like this: "At the ranch I didn't do anything unless I felt the Lord told me to. Jack didn't encourage us to work, only to read the Bible, and after I accepted the Lord that's all I felt like doing. Jack would say, 'This is a place to grow tall, the city is a place to put on the muscle.' There was nothing to distract me there. It was just me and God. There was nobody laying any trips on me, nobody saying, 'Jesus loves you.' The only time they'd answer me about God was if I asked them a question. We could do some work in the fields, but Jack didn't push it. All the work he wanted us to do was turn the pages of the Bible. We didn't even have to do that if we didn't want to. I couldn't have come to God anywhere else because I had a hang-up about authority, as did a lot of people I knew in the counterculture. I didn't have to worry about any authority up there but God.

"The problem was that I remained in an inactive condition when I came back to the city. I lived with an aunt but I wasn't really functioning. I couldn't see that God wanted me to do any work, so I didn't do any. Some of the guys with Moishe would ask, 'Do you want to hand out some tracts with us?' I'd just reply, 'If Father wants me to.'' It was really a bad place to be, not functioning at all for a couple of months. Then I started slipping out of it, getting involved in activities with the other Jews for Jesus. Now, my life is almost all action—action for God.''

As Baruch mentioned, the ranch doesn't exist anymore. After a flood washed them out, Jack and Liz Dunn began traveling around the country, doing other work to which God called them. But despite the short existence of their Oregon retreat, their efforts had an immeasurable impact on our urban, action-oriented ministry in San Francisco. The Jews for Jesus, with their demonstrations, confrontations, and exuberant creative expressions, are in a sense the direct spiritual descendants of the detached, contemplative life of Jack Dunn's ranch.

9 THE TRIBE

"In our society anyone whose religion matters is considered to be too religious. For most people, a religious faith is like a blood type. It's just something you put on an identification card, but it doesn't affect your life very much, except in emergencies."

This observation by Stuart Dauermann reflects a basic complaint of the group which, in the fall of 1970, came to be known as the Jews for Jesus. These young people, ranging in age from the late teens to the middle twenties, were attracted to Jesus not by contemporary, watered-down versions of Christianity, but by His call for a total commitment. They joined a movement, not an organization. Their operational structure, which has many lessons to offer the church as a whole, can best be described as tribal.

The innate impulse to gather into tribal groups is deeply imbedded in the human personality. The popular anthropologist, Robert Ardrey, has pointed out in his book, *The Social Contract,* that for thousands of years men spent most of their waking hours in roving, hunting bands of about eleven individuals each. In those early days, when agriculture and even the bow and arrow were unknown, humans had to learn to work together to kill game, or they perished.

The Jews-for-Jesus movement represents a return to the tribal relationship within the church. The sources of our tribal tendencies are twofold. In the first place, many of our young people came from the hippie subculture, where communal living and extended family units were a way of life. In most of the urban communal pads I've visited, each person has an informal, natural function that satisfies a peculiar need of the group. Some of the hippies are dealers. They bring in money for food and other necessities by selling drugs. Others are poets or artists. They enhance the cultural life of their tribe. If cleanliness occupies a high priority for another communal hippie, he might be the first to help with domestic cleaning chores. The best cooks will also contribute their skills to the welfare of the whole social organism. No matter what an individual's particular "thing" may be, he contributes to the overall *raison d'être* of the group, which is usually just to "be beautiful."

But there's a second, peculiarly Jewish tradition that reinforces our tribal instincts. As I've mentioned, primitive man recognized he

couldn't stand alone against hostile nature. He needed other people
to aid in hunting and to give him a sense of status and the encourage-
ment to develop his own abilities. Jews have been involved in tribal
relationships for centuries because of the need to insure their own
survival as God's chosen people. God called Abraham out of the
urban society of Ur of the Chaldeans and commanded him to assume
a nomadic life. Jews ever since then have maintained an internal
tribal organization, whether they were moving around as itinerant
peddlers or living in the ghettos of Europe and Russia. Despite increasing cultural assimilation, there is still a strong Jewish subculture
in many parts of the United States. It is from this sort of background
that most of our young people have come.

The hippie and Jewish tribal traditions have merged in the Jews-
for-Jesus movement. There are usually about twenty of us at any one
time who belong to our San Francisco core group. The number that
works on any given project is usually even smaller, say around eight.
A primary goal of the primeval hunting band was to get enough food
for the tribe to survive. We are also mobilized to achieve an overriding goal—encounter evangelism. We're "achievement-oriented,"
as Vickie Kress, one of the original Jews for Jesus, put it. Everyone
who is an active member of our core group works, and works hard.
To be accepted as a full participant, a person has to contribute at
least twenty-four hours a week to our activities. The old hunting band
had its chieftain, spear makers, spear throwers, scouts, and medicine
men. We have our leaders, artists, musicians, tract passers, and other
specialists.

There are no formal membership requirements to join the tribe,
because we are not an organization in the conventional sense of the
word. We'll accept any sincere Christian, or sincere seeker after the
truth, who shows a willingness to work. But several attempts by
hostile groups to infiltrate the tribe have forced us to examine more
closely the apparent motives of anyone who expresses an interest in
joining us.

With regard to fulfilling tribal functions, I have told each brother
and sister that those who can work should work. They should not
sit around all day to praise Jesus. This was a radical concept for
many of the hippies. In the past, a person would get saved, throw his
savings into the community pot, and then just sit around and read
the Bible. But I told them they could not deal with most landlords
that way. It was necessary, if they wanted a sustained ministry, to
settle down somewhere and demonstrate an ability to pay regular rent.

Some of them had unemployment money coming in, but I pointed out that their inactivity was bad for their development as Christians. Although it's good to pray and read the Bible, these things tend to deteriorate when a person is not doing something constructive with his time. I encouraged them to get jobs or go to school, and most have bought the advice. Of the core group, two-thirds have either graduated or are attending Bible college. Most are church members in addition to attending synagogue regularly. Accepting responsibility is the key to discipleship.

Our living arrangements range from ordinary homes and apartments to communes. At my suggestion, eight young men and women got permission to live in a vacant church parsonage in return for keeping up the grounds until a new minister arrived. At least one married couple always lives with the group. I believe such arrangements are healthy because the guys behave better when the girls are around and vice versa. This enhances the social development of the tribe.

It has been said that we are organized generally along revolutionary lines because we are trying to change people and situations in a radical fashion. But we are more dynamic in our individual roles than most of the radical paramilitary groups. Any individual Jew for Jesus may wear several hats, depending on the function he is performing at the moment.

My role is that of the tribal leader. I preside over our weekly staff meeting and act as primary spokesman for the press and in major public debates. I'm usually the primary strategist in demonstrations and other confrontations, and I handle the overall coordination for our activities. But I am by no means a dictator who always gets his own way, a Svengali or hypnotist who controls pliable young minds. On the contrary, I am frequently challenged or overridden on ideas I may propose to the group. My role has been described by one of the Jews for Jesus as that of a spiritual elder brother because I have more experience in many Christian matters than the younger people.

My right-hand man is a woman, Steffi Geiser. As my prime adviser, she can usually pick out the flaws in a given plan of action or a piece of literature we propose. Her ability to estimate the potential effect on young people is phenomenal. She has been my co-strategist and expediter in dealing with creative communication.

Steffi and I are very different as individuals. We are both intense perfectionists, but I tend to be shy, quiet, and contemplative, while Steffi is gregarious, winsome, and always making jokes.

Because of her talent for composing songs, drawing, and writing poetry, Steffi has become our art director and is responsible for the illustration and writing of the broadsides and placards we use for demonstrations. We now devote an entire room to our art department. Steffi is assisted by Shelley Korotkin, who is also a good illustrator, although her chief talent is fine painting.

Steffi and I first met in January, 1971. I had been in the San Francisco area for six months and was teaching a regular Bible study in conjunction with Christian World Liberation Front on the campus of the University of California at Berkeley. Steffi had come out here during her winter vacation from the University of Buffalo and a friend had roped her into attending one of my lectures.

"When I first saw Moishe, he was heavier than he is now, and he looked very hokey to me," Steffi commented. "I thought that whole Bible-study thing was very absurd. One girl came over to me and just stared. Her eyes were crossed and she was wearing an old lady's hat and fur coat. The entire experience was bizarre. But I needed a place to stay, and some of the kids in the Bible study invited me to their house. I didn't know it at the time, but Moishe bought food for me and other people who needed it. When I got to the house where these Christian kids were staying, I began to read one of the Bibles they left lying around, partly because they had been nice to me and partly because I was really curious.

"Two days later, on Sunday, I accepted the Lord," she said. "Everybody in the house was really ecstatic about my decision and congratulated me over and over again. I called Moishe and said, 'Mr. Rosen, I accepted Christ.' He said, 'Are you sure?' I said, 'Uh, yeah.' Then he replied, 'That's nice, but we have some people here for dinner. I'll call you on Tuesday.' Frankly, I was expecting him to jump up and down and appear immediately, but he was pretty cool about it. I know now that's his style, and I think it's probably wise because some young people jump into a Christian commitment without thinking through all the implications."

The decision to accept Christ, as Steffi indicated, is not primarily a blind, emotional commitment as far as I am concerned. I always take a wait-and-see attitude, and I don't encourage immediate baptism unless a person is sure of what he is doing. But Steffi was sure, and she started hanging around with us, though she didn't really begin to participate until the summer of 1971.

"I had worked as a designer and illustrator for a firm in New York for a while, and despite the fact that I daily got stoned on pot and acid in the ladies' room at that job, I got some good experience," she recalled. "Moishe asked me to work on a couple of tracts for him, but I kept putting him off because I didn't want the responsibility. Finally, I did one tract, and then another, and another. By June, 1971, I was spending most of my time in the Corte Madera headquarters doing art work."

Steffi lived with us that summer until she started school in the fall at Simpson Bible College. She was graduated from Simpson *summa cum laude* in June, 1973.

Although Steffi has had a key role in making policy for our group, she's not the only one who participates in the decision making. All the Jews for Jesus act as my advisors at one time or another, and I must confess that I have learned more about communication from them than I have been able to teach. Ceil, Steffi, and most of the others are constantly bombarding me with constructive criticism. All my sermons and lessons get a post mortem of, "Maybe you should have said . . . ."

One of these indispensable naggers is Amy Rabinovitz, a bubbly southern belle who serves as our office manager. "I'm probably the office manager because I spend so much time here," she says with a grin. It's not unusual for her to spend twelve to sixteen hours a day doing secretarial work and then attending Bible studies, demonstrations, and singing performances by members of the group. Amy is also a kind of substitute mother for me. I have to have somebody organize my daily schedule or my forward progress comes to a screeching halt, and she is one of the most effective organizers I've ever met.

Amy lived first in Pennsylvania and Wyoming and then moved with her family to Abilene and then to Houston. "Although I was vice-president of a B'nai B'rith chapter and very active in it for several years," she says, "I began to lose my sense of identity as a Jew in Houston and instead began more and more to conform to a primarily gentile community. I went to college for a while. I took a job handling complaints in a camera store, then left school and worked as a secretary in the straight business world. I was always going to cocktail parties, and I especially adored long weekend bashes. I was really happy, having a good time using marijuana and other drugs. My main ambition in life was to marry a millionaire. I had even decided on the quote for my tombstone (from the John O'Hara novel *Ourselves to Know*), 'And all knowledge is, ourselves to know.' "

But an inner yearning to find herself as a Jew kept bothering Amy, and so she decided to emigrate to Israel. She got her passport and plane ticket and finished the other preliminary preparations for the trip. But then she made the fateful decision before she left to try to reconvert a friend named Kathy in Denver who had recently become a Christian.

"I shouted and raged at her as she told me about Jesus," Amy said. Within three months of the time she spoke to her friend Kathy, Amy had made a commitment to Jesus. "I was a believer for several months before I would witness to anyone because of a fear someone would be as nasty to me as I had been to Kathy," Amy recalled.

I met Amy at the Explo '72 rally in Dallas, where she was working for Campus Crusade on prayer and publicity for Explo. When I interviewed her, I told her the hours were long, the pay was miniscule, I was eccentric, and the office was a madhouse. But she wanted the job anyway. More than anything else, she wanted to work in Jewish evangelism.

She joined us as the office manager in California the next month and now she has found that identity she was always seeking before she became a Christian. "I've become more interested in my Jewish heritage, in the things I had done and learned as a child without really understanding them," she explained. "I'd say I'm a true Jew now because Jews are supposed to serve God, and I'm doing that through Christ as He works through me. My love for the Jewish people has grown tremendously and I'm turned on by Jewish music and dancing and have been studying Hebrew again. I studied it for about six years as a child, but forgot most of what I learned."

Another important function in our tribal structure is public relations and Susan Perlman fills that role as our information officer. "I believe the media can be a real ministry," says Susan. "I studied communications in college, and I've always seen power in words. When I came to Christ, I wanted my words to express His message. Moishe asked me what I wanted to do when I came to California. When I said, 'Write,' he pointed to a typewriter and said, 'We've got enough work to keep five writers busy. If you are any good, we'll do everything we can to help.'" Susan has now been published by *Eternity* and other Christian periodicals.

Susan brought some unique experience from New York, when she joined us in June, 1972. She had formerly worked for Blaine Thompson Company, Inc., an agency which handles much of the advertising for the New York entertainment industry. She also wrote advertising copy for J. C. Penney. We put Susan to work on publicity and media relations and she became our information officer.

Unlike the others, Susan was never a hippie, but then she wasn't quite straight either. Her life had been fast and exciting. Her personable smile had gotten her more dates to the best places than most girls. She became a Christian after she approached folk singer Larry Norman on the street and asked him if he bleached his hair to get it so blonde. In the ensuing conversation he witnessed to her about Jesus, and she made a Christian commitment soon afterwards.

Susan usually charms the city-desk editor or news director into covering a story or interviewing one of the Jews for Jesus. I would have thought that the media would tire of our demonstrations and pro-Jesus statements a long time ago, but Susan has managed to keep them interested in the strange notion (to some folks it is strange, anyway) that Jews can believe in Jesus and still remain Jews.

Susan also was involved with street theater in New York and has brought valuable experience to our street-theater group. As the assistant director, she works under Jh'an Moskowitz, our drama director.

When we plan a demonstration or participate in a protest with other members of the Jewish community, we notify the media to give them pertinent details and quotable statements. Susan follows up with a briefing bulletin and news releases on the events. We are constantly on the lookout for topics that will be interesting enough for newspaper, radio, and television interviews, so that we can get our message out to an otherwise secular audience.

We cannot always rely on the press, however, because at times pressure is exerted by Jewish community leaders to keep our activities out of the newspapers and off television. As a result, we take our own photographers to record the events for possible later use. Glenda Alford is our regular photographer, and her pictures have appeared in *Newsweek* and other publications.

Steffi, Amy, and Susan might be called my staff officers because they are primarily involved in planning our activities and helping me coordinate strategy. But when the action starts on the streets, a different group takes over—our tribal group leaders who control demonstrations and other confrontations.

Because we frequently find ourselves in tight situations, it is necessary when we go to the streets and on the campuses, that we operate with considerable thoughtful restraint and discipline. Our tactics call for us to be visible and articulate and open to personal encounters; but we realize that the particular way in which we manifest Christ is one that sometimes causes people to vent their resentment and anger at us.

The group leaders are Tuvya Zaretsky, who spent more than a year in Israel and then joined us in September, 1972; Bruce Skoropinski, one of our few *goyim,* who leads the North Beach demonstrations against the topless-bottomless bars; and Baruch Goldstein, the alumnus of the Oregon ranch, who is my main lieutenant on out-of-town trips.

Baruch has also been especially valuable in managing our street testimony. He has become so enthusiastic in passing out tracts and getting others to do the same that frequently I have to caution him about the cost of paper. He's a natural leader of men, a dynamic and engaging preacher, and his Bible-college training has given him a good grasp of Scripture. Baruch has virtually taken charge of all literature distribution and scouts out opportunities for us to present the gospel.

When we go out on the streets, whether to demonstrate or just to take a walk, each of us usually will take along a handful of broadsides to distribute to other pedestrians. Two of the most avid tract passers, though they fulfill other important functions in the tribe as well, have been Sam Nadler and Vickie Kress. Their backgrounds are good illustrations of the variety of experience we can offer in helping confused, mixed-up young people identify with Christ.

Sam knew some of the people who stayed at Jack Dunn's ranch in Oregon. But he came to Christ by another route that took him through a frightening and satanically-controlled realm of the counterculture. Sam was drafted into the army and was shipped off to Vietnam at the height of the war. He made it back in one piece and in his stateside duty station, he managed to establish a lucrative drug business. He decided he wanted to deal only in "high class" drugs, so he became a "clean dealer" who trafficked in marijuana, hashish, and psychedelics, not the hard stuff like heroin. While he was still in the army, Sam also set up a loan-sharking operation which netted him interest at the rate of about 600 percent annually.

"Both the drug dealing and the lending operation were rotten things to do," he said, "but I didn't see anything wrong with them at the time; and I was doing very well financially. When I got out of the service, I believed that drugs were for everyone. After attending Georgia State University for a semester, I dropped out and started traveling across the country in a van, selling drugs when I needed the money. It was one continuous party. I'd sometimes have eighteen people in the van, with lots of girl friends, all that I wanted. It was the All-American dream."

Sam stopped for a while in San Francisco, then moved to a small town in northern California to manage a saloon. He formed a band and played his harmonica and composed songs to his heart's content. Then things started to go wrong. He and his girl friend of the moment split up, his house burned down, and he lost his job.

"Some friends of mine and I had staged an acid orgy with five Indian chicks we picked up, but when we got back to our place, it was nothing but ashes," he explained. "I decided the time had come to go back to San Francisco. It would be Jamaica for the winter. But again, I ran into trouble. I couldn't sell my van, and the novelty of the Jamaica idea soon wore off. I had started a nice drug business again, and so I decided to stay in the Bay area for a while.

"One day, in the fall of 1971, a girl I knew started telling me about some people she had met who called themselves Jews for Jesus. I said, 'Okay, I guess everybody needs a label. But what will they think of next?' She kept pushing me to go to a Bible study with her, and finally I agreed. I met Moishe there, and frankly I was flabbergasted when he said he believed in a personal God. 'You actually talk to Him, like you talk to me?' I asked. It was all so ridiculous."

Sam said that he believed at the time that real spiritual truth lay in the occult, particularly in the *I Ching* and astrology. "I was certain that there was a spiritual power that I could tap," he said. "Moishe had said that personal prayer worked for him, and because that seemed like part of the same bag I was into, I decided to try it. I still hadn't been able to get rid of my car, and so I said conversationally to God, 'Can you help me get rid of it?' Soon afterwards, I sold the car, and I sensed somehow my prayer had been answered. I also found that the *I Ching* would give me the same reading over and over again: 'You'll meet the great man.' I got in the habit of walking up to people and asking, 'Who's the great man?' With amazing frequency, they would answer, 'Jesus Christ.' But at that point, Jesus was still a lark with me."

Unimpressed with these encounters with Christianity, Sam decided to throw himself heart and soul into the occult. "I could actually find out what people were doing in an adjoining room just by getting a hexogram from coins. Then a heavy thing happened one night. I was sitting in the kitchen, rapping with some friends, and a strange presence or feeling filled the room. It grasped each of us to the point that we sat up straight, completely alert. We had a sense that something was about to happen. Although none of us were Christians, one guy started talking about Jesus. He talked for about ten or fifteen minutes, and the rest of us were transfixed. Then he got up and just as he left, another non-Christian friend came into the room and took up where the first guy had left off. Then the feeling seemed to dissipate, and we became aware of sounds outside the room. The first thing we heard was Billy Graham on the radio. He was saying, 'Never before have so many young people been turning to Christ.' "

This experience made Sam get serious. He went to his room and asked God to make Himself real, to reveal Himself if He were really there. But nothing happened immediately. A few days later, Sam started attending classes on how to use the occult to gain power over other people. One lecturer said, "This is black magic I'm going to show you now. You can learn to control yourself and other people. You can communicate with the spirit world for whatever purpose you like, whether good or bad, moral or immoral."

"A spade was finally being called a spade," Sam said. "That night I was shown that I was involved in something evil. I could now sense the difference between good and evil, between God and Satan. I knew I had been following Satan. I went home and began to sing every song I had ever written, and I thought, 'These are all the good things I've ever done. I'm going to sing them to You, God.' Then some of my neighbors started drifting in, heroin dealers and such, and it dawned on me the kind of social circle I was in. They filled the entire house that night. I knew Satan was present, and I became more and more frightened."

Sam turned down the drugs that his friends offered him that evening, but he practically had to fight them off. "It was a frightful night, trying to turn around, change my ways all at once. I can't tell you how sure I was that Satan was there, right there. You could feel the evil, the heaviness of it. I just knew I had to have Jesus in my life. I went to the stairs, fell to my knees, and asked Him into my life. As soon as I did it, as soon as I prayed, people started leaving. They had given no indication before that they were ready to go. It was God acting, no question in my mind. I was comforted, but I realized that I couldn't live in that house anymore. The people there were very much under Satan's control, into his trip."

The next day, Sam sought out some Christians he knew and got in touch with me through them. Before the day was out, he had joined the tribe. Within a month of that time, he was enrolled in Simpson Bible College.

Vickie Kress, another of our key tract passers, came to Christ by a different route which only skirted the hippie movement. She fell in love with a college classmate in New York, and they both dropped out and hitchhiked to San Francisco. But then she and her boyfriend decided to split, and Vickie found herself doing file-clerk work and hating it.

"My boyfriend really got into the hippie scene—pot, free love—but I found it unattractive," she said. "We had a communications gap, so he went his way and I went mine. But because I still wanted to be able to relate to him, I decided to look for sensational things to do, too. I ended up doing the same things he did. I took pot and even had one mescaline trip and studied astrology. I held what I thought of as a dull job for two years. After that, I returned to New York to join a commune in which my former boyfriend was staying, but I found he had flipped out from heavy drugs."

Disillusioned and deeply depressed, Vickie eventually left the commune. Shortly afterward, through Miriam Sleichter, she was introduced to me and some other Jewish Christians at the Beth Sar Shalom center. After several lengthy conversations and a lot of thought and Bible reading, she became a believer and joined the original group that accompanied me to California in the summer of 1970.

We Jews for Jesus, then, are a tribe of contrasting individuals who have been welded together by one primary goal: We want to let nonbelievers, and especially young Jews, know what Jesus has done for us. We are not, however, a separate, isolated sect. Most of us also belong to nearby churches, where we serve on committees, teach Sunday-school classes, and participate in musical programs. In one church there are representatives from our tribe, a tribe of gentile hippie Christians, and a third tribe of straight Christians whose main contacts are with the local business community. The Jews for Jesus are constantly in touch with these other tribes, and we've learned to help and reinforce one another, as one in the body of Christ. Each tribe makes a contribution to the worldwide spiritual "nation" of the church through the local congregation; but at the same time each has its own special role in working outside the congregation to carry the gospel to non-Christians.

10 CONFRONTATION TACTICS—
POWERS OF DARKNESS

The Jews-for-Jesus movement exists for one purpose—to serve God by confronting the world with the claims of Christ. In the United States, evangelism for the most part is carried on in the churches or at rallies which are attended mostly by Christians. If the church were successful in its evangelistic efforts, it wouldn't be necessary to conduct revival meetings on sanctified premises. Our model for telling the Good News is the Book of Acts. After Jesus' disciples received the baptism of the Holy Spirit in Acts, they didn't linger in the Upper Room. They went down to the streets where the people were and preached about the wonderful works of God, according to the biblical account.

In our contemporary society, we have conditioned our young people to think that they are participating if they sit and listen to what is being said. From the time a child enters the first grade, he is encouraged to pay attention to his teachers, to be an academic sponge that soaks up knowledge. He sits through college, through church. He has to use his seat instead of his feet as a way of showing commitment. Many church members think that they are doing the work of God by sitting through four or five prayer meetings, Bible studies, sermons, and committee meetings each week. If I could tell the church anything about Christian service, it would be, "Get off your seat and onto your feet."

Or, as the Bible says:

> How beautiful upon the mountains are the feet of him that bringeth good tidings, that publisheth peace; that bringeth good tidings of good, that publisheth salvation; that saith unto Zion, Thy God reigneth!
>
> Isaiah 52:7

Our strategy is to have each person make a statement about God and His wonderful works of redemption. Our young evangelists tell the wonderful stories of redemption from dope, the devil, depression, and disillusionment. Since the Jews-for-Jesus movement has become more prominent, there have been many who have approached us and volunteered their services. We can't accept most of these people, even

though they are willing to pay their own way, but those we do accept
are initiated into our tribal life in a very simple way. Either Baruch
Goldstein or I will take them out on the streets, hand them a stack of
broadsides, and take a stack for ourselves. We then begin handing the
literature out to the crowds of pedestrians. If the new volunteer is the
kind of person we want, he'll try passing the tracts as well. Usually
he's surprised to see that more people accept the literature than refuse
it. Frequently he becomes enthusiastic and excited. That's the kind
of person we want.

We place a high value on communicative skills. But no matter how
many talents a person might have, or how much education, if he is
not willing to stand with us on the streets as a witness for Christ, he
can't become part of the Jews-for-Jesus thing. No matter how busy
my own schedule might be, I always manage to get out sometime
during the week to witness on the streets. Holy boldness is not a
natural thing. It takes spirit-filled people to set aside their dignity and
humble themselves and risk the abuse that confrontation might bring.

The Jews for Jesus have become controversial because of confrontation tactics. Most of the pictures that have been published in maga-
zines show us with placards conducting a demonstration in front of
this place or that. But demonstrating is only one of our means of
confrontation.

My dictionary defines confrontation as "to stand or come in front
of, stand or meet facing." That's what we want—to face people. We
don't want to get in their way or aggravate them into accepting Christ,
but rather to make ourselves available for anyone who may be interested in learning about Jesus. Our demonstrations in front of the
topless-bottomless clubs are often misunderstood. We're not there to
protest what's going on inside, but to *attest* to the fact that Christ
alone can satisfy the longing of the human heart.

The fact that our presence may hurt the bars is incidental to our
main purpose. We want to awaken the consciences of individuals so
that they remember there's a God in heaven who cares, or a Christ
who died for them, or a transcendent morality that they might have
heard about in church on a previous Sunday.

For us, confrontation means that we have to be viable, visible, and
vocal. God has given us a high degree of enthusiasm, of spiritual via-
bility. We rejoice to serve Him and we want to show it. On the streets
we look alive, not merely because we're young, but because of the new
life-force that we've received in the Holy Spirit. In my own experience,
the Holy Spirit not only gives me God's Word to speak, but also gives

me the ability to be patient with those who don't want to hear. The Holy Spirit has helped me to endure what others would regard as abuse.

Our tactics of visual confrontation take several forms. We have shirts and jackets with our slogans: "Jews for Jesus" or "Jesus Made Me Kosher," or in the case of Bruce Skoropinski, who is the former president of the student body at Simpson College and a Gentile, "Jews and Others for Jesus." When we demonstrate we use placards with these slogans and wear our identity on our backs because we want people to come and ask. If our slogan were "Christians for Jesus," I don't think we would get nearly as many inquiries.

As crazy and radical as we may look, there's a certain method to our sartorial madness. In street clothes, denims, or informal dress we're able to identify with the culture and age group of the people we most want to encounter. On the West Coast many people are comfortable in jeans and weirdly decorated clothing. But denims are not a compulsory uniform with us. When I preach in church I manage to get out an old suit. I feel that one should dress according to the dictates of the situation and I've even been known to wear a clerical collar and vestments to speak and conduct services in the more liturgical churches.

We usually choose the street or campus as our place of confrontation, not the pulpit or the pew. And vocal confrontation for us is not merely shouting slogans and chants, but being able to verbalize our feelings with conviction and tell them to others. After each street action we have a period of debriefing which includes prayer and a discussion of what we've learned. In addition, each person in the group relates questions that have been asked him, and we then talk over possible answers. For example, at one session one of our volunters said, "This guy asked me how much I get paid to evangelize. I told him one thousand dollars a convert, and if he'd convert, I'd split my prize with him."

"Why did you tell him that?" asked another. "Why couldn't you give him a straight answer?"

"Because it wasn't a straight question. The Bible says 'Answer a fool according to his folly, lest he be wise in his own conceit'" (Proverbs 26:5).

Our confrontations frequently involve direct, unequivocal communication, but since such an approach can produce conflict and misunderstanding, we always try to be loving and accepting, as well as honest toward the other person. Down on Market Street I was handing out broadsides, and a young . . . well, I couldn't tell if the person was a boy or girl, approached me. The dress was female, but the walk didn't seem quite at home in high heels. When I heard the voice, I knew that the individual was a male. He asked, "Do you believe that homosexuals are going to hell?"

"Yes," I said, "but I believe all those who choose to serve self and not God are guilty of sin and are going to hell. Only those who have committed themselves to Christ can escape the penalty of sin. But let me ask you a question. Do you believe in hell?"

"We homosexuals are living in hell now and it's a hell made by people like you," he replied.

"Wait a minute," I said. "You're the one who approached me with a question. I didn't stop you. I have nothing against you. The question you have to ask yourself is whether or not God is satisfied with the life you've chosen for yourself."

"The problem is you with your literature. You're promoting a morality that I can't accept because I have a different physical nature. It's not natural for me to try to be like you."

I pointed out that as a natural man, a non-Christian, he was not able to perceive the things of God. But I also told him that God could give him a supernatural power that would enable him to follow a Christian morality.

Jimmy, who called himself Janie, was interested when I mentioned the power to be different. He had never been satisfied to think of himself as being a helpless victim of environmental conditioning. That afternoon, he made a decision to bring God into his life. I haven't seen Jimmy again, but I did get a letter that said that he was straight, going to church, and dating a girl that he hoped to marry.

"Well," I mused recently with a friend, "many psychiatrists give up on homosexuals, but an encounter with God in a brief few minutes can sure change things. God used the confrontation on the streets because that's where He found Jimmy."

Effective evangelism often takes place within an arena of confrontation; yet many Christians hesitate to evangelize simply because they know that confrontation occasionally produces conflict, and they hope to avoid the unpleasantness that *might* occur. But if we're not willing to endure possible difficulties and risk possible rejection, we'll never be able to achieve much for God or experience much spiritual satisfaction.

When the movie *Jesus Christ Superstar* came to town, several of us went to see it. I liked the music, enjoyed the staging, and found it to be an enjoyable experience. Then I felt thoroughly guilty because it portrayed Jesus as a shrieking simpleton who wandered about spouting pious platitudes. He complained that His disciples didn't love Him enough and wondered if posterity would remember Him. Several of the other Jews for Jesus didn't like the movie at all. But one thing we all agreed on was that it didn't represent the Jesus we knew. It was a misrepresentation of the Jesus that I have come to know and love, a misrepresentation of the gospel message.

We decided to demonstrate, to tell the moviegoers what we knew about the Lord of Lords and King of Kings, the one who had ransomed us. We knew that by demonstrating we would probably provoke a confrontation. Sure enough, some people regarded us as a bunch of humorless oddballs, but through television and the newspapers, our testimony about the real Jesus reached others.

We didn't tell people not to see the movie; we told them where we felt the movie was wrong and some listened. Since the theater patrons were obviously interested in the subject of Jesus, we used our demonstration to add to their knowledge. We tried to be good-natured as we sang and chanted and smiled and passed out our position sheet. We weren't angry because the film didn't show our Saviour in biblical terms; we don't expect the world to always do that. That's *our* job! The film introduced the subject to the minds of people, and we took the occasion to elaborate.

For the past few years I've been reading the writings of political radicals. Most of their methods and techniques are inappropriate for Christian communication, but I've learned a lot from these thinkers, particularly from Saul Alinsky. Among other things, he taught me, in his book, *Rules for Radicals,* that it's important for demonstrators to anticipate what concessions their opposition might be willing to make in return for stopping public protests.

Alinsky argues that if protestors would do some intelligent second-guessing they could avoid being caught off guard and would be in a better position to formulate demands ahead of time. After we got involved in the antismut campaign in San Francisco's North Beach section, we suspected that our presence might drive away the business of the topless bars. With Alinsky's principle in mind, we decided that if they asked us what we wanted in return for staying away, we would request the right to preach the gospel inside the bars.

Sure enough, our protests made them want to give us concessions. When we informed them that we wanted to preach the gospel in the bars, all of the bar owners turned us down at first. Finally, one owner, who was getting desperate, invited us in and we gave a show he'll probably never forget. We filled up the place with a bunch of Jesus people and asked several Christian leaders to help us preach. One of them was the author and evangelist Hal Lindsey, who came up from Los Angeles. The customers who had come into the bar expecting to see some titillating dancing just gaped in disbelief. I was standing next to the bar, and one patron said, "What kind of act is this? I don't like it when they make fun of religion."

"They're not making fun," I replied. "They really believe what they're saying."

"Why are they preaching here?"

"Because they think that you need it, I guess," I answered with a smile.

"I think you're right," he said. Then he walked over to pray with one of the preachers.

Needless to say, we were never invited back because we ran off most of the drinking customers. The bar owner apparently felt it was better to lose a little business from our demonstrations than to forfeit an entire evening's liquor by letting us preach.

As the incident described in the first chapter shows, the clubs sometimes prefer to use violence rather than to entreat us with words. On one occasion Sam Nadler was marching in front of one of the bars trying to manage a placard and hand out literature at the same time. One of his tracts read:

> Topless, bottomless, nothingness . . . . Here you are at North Beach. If you have a superb imagination or enough liquor maybe you can make yourself believe that you're not just a creeping, peeping Tom. [There we inserted an illustration of a man looking at someone through the window.] The barkers smile, the girls smile, the devil smiles. It's not that they're really friendly. They're all amused. You are the evening's entertainment. YOU ARE THE JOKE.

Besides balancing the placard and handing out the pamphlets, Sam did some rather loud testifying and preaching. When he got to the conclusion of his testimony he said, "God can even save these barkers if they turn to Him."

That was too much for one barker. He went inside, brought out a man who was obviously inebriated, and pointed toward Sam. The drunk started menacingly in Sam's direction.

"I could see the guy coming and I thought 'Well, time to stand up for Christ,' " Sam recalled. "He was mean and big and as I pulled out a piece of literature to hand him, he reared back and then, WHAM, the blow knocked me down. But I got right back up. Without really thinking I said, 'God bless you.' The guy backed off and sneered. Then I said, 'Jesus will forgive you for that. God really loves you.' The guy just stood there and scowled at me, and Moishe, who had been standing nearby, went to call the police. My jaw was really in pain. I guess the world would have expected me to fight back, but that's not our way. We believe in passive resistance. Before Jesus, I always fought back and that was the first time I ever said, 'God bless you' to someone who slugged me. I never really thought through what I would do if someone attacked me. We've just tried to condition ourselves to be nonviolent and then rely on God to help us act the right way."

Turning the other cheek is a confrontation. It's a show of strength. To an attacker, it is the taunt that he doesn't have the ability to make the Christian cower. We want to stay near those who choose to cause us pain and who would slap us out of their presence. Our objective is to demonstrate we have the strength to endure an assault without anger toward those who would hurt. Turning the other cheek is a reminder to the bully that he cannot intimidate us by violence; but most of all it is a declaration that we believe our strength comes from a superior Source and that we have the power to forgive.

One result of the demonstrations was a close relationship Sam was able to cultivate with one of the barkers, whom I'll call Joe. He was a Christian who, by his own admission, had backslidden so far from God that he had not only gone deeply into drug use and smut promotion, but had another ominous crime hanging over his head.

"When I saw the Jews for Jesus demonstrating down there, right across the street from me, it made my own dissatisfaction worse," Joe explained. "What could I say to the Lord? I'd been hiding, dodging Him. I had received the Lord once, and I knew that I had to make an effort to go back to Him. One day when I wasn't working I decided to hitchhike to see my wife. We had been separated after only a few months of marriage, but not before I had introduced her to shooting heroin. God was working on me as I stood out there on the street and I found myself praying that God would send me a Christian. This guy driving a van stopped, and just as I got into the seat next to him, he handed me a Jews-for-Jesus tract. It was Sam. I was really shocked. All I could do was say out loud, 'Wow, Lord, that was what I was praying for.' Sam said he usually didn't pick up hitchhikers at that location because the turnoff was only a few blocks ahead, but somehow he felt led to stop that day."

"The fact that I happened by at that time and felt moved to stop, that had to be God acting in answer to Joe's prayer," Sam said. "We prayed and talked before I dropped him off and we kept in touch for a couple of months."

Joe was still not willing to rededicate his life to God, however. "One night Tuvya and Amy were passing out broadsides at North Beach. I walked over and asked if they knew Sam and chatted briefly. But it was hard for me to get out of the devil's grip. I continued to work as a barker and encourage people to come inside to see the sex show, but I became more and more aware that I was working for Satan and selling his product. The people who operated the club practiced black magic. They also had a big cocaine operation. I suppose my drug habit was one of the main things that kept me from returning to the Lord, but something else that was bothering me was even more serious. I had murdered a man in another state a couple of years before, and though I wasn't even a suspect in that crime, I knew that if I let God take over again I'd have to give myself over to the authorities. Nobody had ever learned about my crime or even discovered the body. For all I knew I was home free except for God."

Joe finally attended one of our Bible studies. I spoke on Jesus as the Friend who was willing to make the ultimate sacrifice to lay down His life for those He loved. Joe told Sam after the meeting that he was going to turn himself in on the murder charge. Sam stayed with him throughout the whole ordeal of the next few days. Joe had to notify the FBI, convince them that he wasn't some sort of quack, and then prepare for the inevitable prison term. Sam was always there, advising and encouraging. Joe is now serving a life sentence in a state prison, but is continuing his loyalty to the Lord, witnessing and telling others about Christ.

If our demonstrations at North Beach don't produce another result I think we've been justified just with the change that occurred in Joe's life. He has become an instrument that God can use and that's what the objective of our tribe is. We are not a drug-abuse center or a counseling agency or a social-action organization, but if in spreading the good word about Jesus we also fulfill some of those other roles—and we invariably do—that's even better.

These antismut demonstrations are an important part of our ministry, but another kind of confrontation has even more serious implications for each of us as individuals. I'm referring to the trials and tribulations we face in trying to relate to the Jewish community.

11 CONFRONTATION TACTICS—
THE JEWISH COMMUNITY

"You're not Jews anymore! You've joined the enemy, and we don't want you around!"

A response like this from a hotheaded Jewish leader is a common occurrence when the Jews for Jesus appear at a distinctively Jewish function. Even though we don't wear anything that would identify us as Jews for Jesus or make any attempt to initiate religious conversation when we attend most synagogue services or other Jewish activities, some Jews consistently try to exclude us because of our faith. Such rejections raise a basic question that most people cannot answer: What, exactly, *is* a Jew?

The question of Jewish identity has always plagued the Jewish community, especially in recent times when so many Jews have decided they don't need God or the serious religious observances He commanded in the Scriptures. According to the *Halakah,* or the body of Jewish law, a person is a Jew if his mother was Jewish or if he converts to Judaism. My mother was Jewish and the same goes for the other Jews for Jesus, so we're Jewish under the law. We may be heretics in the eyes of some Jewish leaders, but we're still Jewish. The problem we face is that not all rabbis and other Jewish leaders are willing to accept us as Jews.

With the decline of Jewish religious interest, many Jews have tried to define their identity in cultural rather than religious terms. Or they may dodge the identity issue, as the Israeli Supreme Court did a few years ago when Oswald Rufeisen, an Orthodox Jew who had converted to Catholicism, applied for Israeli citizenship under the Law of Return. Although Rufeisen, also known as "Brother Daniel," could trace his Jewishness through his mother, the court by a majority vote declined to accept him as a citizen because of his faith. Conceding that in technical religious terms Brother Daniel might still be a Jew, the court nevertheless refused to pass on that issue.

In the original biblical sense, a Jew is a person who is an heir to the covenants God made with Abraham, Moses, and David. For the Jewish male, the symbol of this *bris,* or covenant, is circumcision. I have to agree with one writer, James Yaffe, in his *The American Jews,* who said, "The physical nature of this rite is significant; it suggests that there is something irreversible about entering into the covenant, something that can't be affected by a mere change of belief." The eternal nature of God's covenant with His chosen people has been expressed by a variety of authorities on the subject. Roger Kahn has noted in his book *The Passionate People,* "One cannot stop being Jewish by choice; personal choice is irrelevant to Jewishness. The covenant between God and Abraham, renewed between God and Moses, is what binds Jews, according to the [*Halakah.*] The binding is eternal." Kahn highlights the issue that confronts the Jews for Jesus when he declares, "A Jew who joins the Roman Catholic Church sins, but so does a Jew who simply neglects to pray. Neither condition alters the individual's Jewishness. It makes him a bad Jew to be sure . . . . But his Jewishness is unaffected."

Of course, I would take issue with Kahn when he says that a Jewish Christian is a "bad Jew." On the contrary, a Jew who has accepted Jesus is the only good Jew. All other Jews who fail to obey one small part of the *Halakah* are bad Jews or heretics. Even those who are reasonably conscientious, Orthodox Jews fall short by this test. They're practicing Christless Christianity, looking fruitlessly for the Messiah who has already come, wrestling with a *Halakah* that has already been fulfilled. But because I recognize Christ as *Hamashiach,* or Messiah, God no longer judges my righteousness by the law. Jesus has made me and every other Jewish Christian kosher.

Despite the fact that the *Halakah* and every authoritative definition of Jewishness is on our side, many Jewish leaders and rabbis still don't accept us as members of their community. We like to participate in Jewish fairs and demonstrations, and sometimes a rabbi will object. Hostility never deters us, but why do we want to go where we're not wanted? The Jewish people have always had a key role in God's plan for mankind, and we're not about to let some misinformed rabbi excommunicate us from God's covenant. The Apostle Paul was quite adamant about his identity as a Jew: "For I also am an Israelite, of the seed of Abraham, of the tribe of Benjamin," he declared in Romans 11:1. He was specific and unequivocal about his ancestry and birthright, and so are we.

Contrary to what some Jews think, our purpose in relating to the Jewish community involves more than just evangelism. I'm an evangelist both by profession and by interest. My ministry is similar to that of a guy who loves to play tennis. If I could, I'd spend all my time doing it. But my Jewishness isn't simply the bait on a Christian hook to catch Jewish fish. It's authentic.

Unfortunately, some Jewish leaders have refused to recognize the genuineness of our Jewishness. They have chosen instead to yield to an innate, emotional hostility to Christians and have tried to exclude us from their community. Because we won't stand such unfair and illegal attacks on our rights, we occasionally find it necessary to turn our confrontation tactics toward other Jews in an effort to point out the error of their ways.

Sometimes, the confrontation may involve a little repartee on the street. Baruch Goldstein has come to some definite conclusions about his own Jewishness, so he was ready to respond when a Jewish fellow accosted him at a North Beach demonstration and said gruffly, "You Jewish?"

"Yeah," Baruch replied.

"Well, let's hear your rap!"

"I don't have any rap. What are you talking about?"

"Come on, come on, let's hear your rap," the fellow pressed. "You say you're Jewish. You have a Jewish mother?"

"Yeah, and I've been circumcized too, you want to see?" Baruch retorted.

The young Jewish man backed off, shaking his head. "No, that's okay. I believe you."

Baruch was just trying to shock the guy, make him think, and this sort of approach is usually effective in a one-to-one confrontation. But when other Jews organize to challenge us, our response becomes more complex. The usual ploy that Jewish leaders use is to attempt to curb our freedom of speech. In a recent incident in New York City, for example, representatives of certain segments of the Jewish community banded together to stage a telephone campaign against a television program entitled "Jews for Jesus," which was scheduled to be aired over a local station. The station succumbed to the pressure, and the program was cancelled. These same people try to exert pressure to keep us from speaking to Jewish groups or participating in many Jewish community activities.

Most non-Jews I've talked to find such attacks on the basic human rights of freedom of expression and religion an ironic and rather outrageous reversal of position for the traditionally liberal Jewish community. One observer, James Yaffe, has commented, "Liberalism is the American Jew's lay religion." But Yaffe notes that there's a double motive for this liberalism: On the one hand, Jews have a deep-seated

belief in unselfish idealism and the importance of social welfare. But
at the same time, in evaluating each civil-liberties position, they ask,
"Is it good for the Jews?" Jews have been particularly outspoken in
defense of freedom of speech because they know that, as Yaffe says,
"The society that suppresses free speech may end up forcing Jews to
give up their religion."

Can you imagine the reaction if Roman Catholics tried to keep a
Jewish or Protestant program off the air? The Jews would be the first
to scream bloody murder. But now the roles have changed. The Jews
have always been on the outside trying to get into the mainstream of
society. They were the have-nots who fought tooth and nail to have
occupational, political, and social doors opened to minorities, including themselves. Now Jewish society has become part of the establishment. It seems that high-minded liberalism dissolves into suppression
when the Jews are confronted with a deviant minority inside their own
deviant minority. The Jews for Jesus are advocating a religion that's
not acceptable to many Jewish leaders, and this fact poses a very
serious question. Every Jew in this country is going to have to look
back on Jewish history and ask, "Do we really mean all we've been
saying about free speech, the right to be heard, the right of dissent, and
the right to be different?" Do they really mean it? We are obviously
Jews, and we are claiming the place that Jewish principles say we
should have.

The issue is potentially quite embarrassing, for a lot of Gentiles are
beginning to say, "Hey, you Jews don't believe in censorship on television. Why are you keeping these Jews for Jesus off the air? Why
don't you let them join your public community functions? You Jews
stand for the right of minorities to be included, regardless of their
beliefs. And you've always said a person should not be condemned
because of his religion, that he should be evaluated on his merits as a
person." As the Jews-for-Jesus movement becomes more widely
known, the Jewish community will be confronted more and more with
these questions, and they're not easy to answer.

Our strategy for combatting these censorship attempts is based on
one of Saul Alinsky's rules for have-not groups like ours: "Make the
enemy live up to their own book of rules." I wouldn't characterize our
fellow Jews as the "enemy," but they are often the opposition. Our
purpose is to create situations where they can see the moral inconsistency of their position.

The groundwork for one such confrontation was laid in the spring
of 1973 when a woman named Margaret called our office and said

she wanted to find out more about Jesus and the Jews for Jesus. Amy Rabinovitz went over to visit her, and Margaret almost immediately said she wanted to learn how to become a Christian. Amy witnessed to her about Jesus and explained the steps to salvation, and Margaret said she was interested but she wanted to talk to someone a little older. Amy arranged for an appointment with me, but after the interview with her I didn't know exactly what to think. Because she expressed an interest in working with us, I asked her to do some errands for us. We didn't take her into our confidence, however, because we still weren't sure of her intentions.

Margaret had dropped by the office one day when Amy got a call from one of the leaders in our local Jewish community asking us to help staff some booths that were going to be set up at a Jerusalem Fair to commemorate Israel's twenty-fifth anniversary. We agreed because we enjoy participating in Jewish activities. Margaret left and we didn't hear from her again, but we did get another call from the Jewish leader who had invited us to the fair. He said one of the leading rabbis in San Francisco had called and ordered him and the other fair organizers not to allow the Jews for Jesus to participate in the fair.

We began to wonder how this particular rabbi could have known about our participation, and then Amy mentioned that Margaret had overheard her conversation about the booths. We decided that Margaret must have been the source of the leak, but we couldn't understand exactly what her role was. Despite the cold shoulder, Amy and some of the others decided they would like to participate in the fair anyhow.

"I called up the fair office and volunteered some friends and myself as guides," Amy recalled. "They didn't ask me if I believed in Jesus and I didn't mention it. They needed guides and were happy to have us. Miriam Nadler, Marcia Goldstein, Bruce Skoropinski, and I went down the night of the fair, and we were dressed in Israeli-type clothes, without any Jews-for-Jesus buttons or identification. The fair officials gave us credentials as guides and assigned us to distribute maps of the displays for the fair. I had been standing at my post for a few minutes when who should strut in but Margaret—leading a contingent from the Jewish Defense League."

Amy wasn't given much time to get her bearings before Margaret walked over and demanded, "What are you doing here?"

"Oh, I'm smiling and handing out maps and being nice to people," Amy answered sweetly.

One of Margaret's male companions then approached Amy and said, "Are you Amy Rabinovitz?"

"Yes. Who are you?" Amy questioned.

"My name is Meir . . . Kahane . . . ," the man said.

Amy had never met Kahane, the international leader of the militant JDL, but from photos she'd seen she knew that this man wasn't Kahane. Although she tried to be nonchalant and ignore them, several JDL people surrounded her and asked, "Are you a member of Beth Sar Shalom?"

"Huh? What do you want?" Amy stalled, trying to figure out what to do.

"Beth Sar Shalom, the Jewish-Christian organization. Are you a member?"

"I don't think they have memberships, do they?" she responded. "How do you join them?" Amy tried to walk away to get the security guard, but they blocked her and surrounded her menacingly.

"Are you a Jew for Jesus?" one asked.

"Look, I've got better things to do than talk to you," Amy said. Seeing Margaret standing a few feet away, Amy said, "Margaret, your friends are really freaking me out. What's going on?"

"We hate you," Margaret replied coldly.

Amy was beginning to realize that things weren't going to get any better, when another girl walked up, shoved a pendant depicting a clenched fist and a star of David into Amy's face and demanded, "Do you know what this is?" Amy knew it was the JDL symbol. "Well, we don't want you handing out this information," the girl continued. We don't want you working here. Turn in your badge, right now! I mean it. I won't let you do this. I'll bash your head in if I have to."

With the JDL girl clutching her arm, Amy went up to the security guard and complained, "These people are threatening me; help me."

The guard just shrugged and said, "Don't hurt her." Then he turned to Amy and said, "If you get hurt, let me know."

Amy finally told the JDL people she would turn in her badge, but only to an authorized fair official. Within moments a rabbi appeared who identified himself as the head of the fair. "I figured they could be up to tricks, so I asked to see his driver's license," Amy explained. "His name was on all the official badges, so I realized he must be authentic. By that time there was a large crowd of people standing around, and they were all shouting different things. Some were just curious, but most were yelling 'She's a Jew for Jesus,' 'She's handing out Jesus material here,' 'She's an infiltrator,' and things like that.

"Finally the rabbi asked me to turn in my badge for the peace of the fair. I explained that I wasn't distributing anything but the maps I had been given, but some of the JDL people had complained that I was giving out 'subversive' literature. Nothing I said was helping, so I finally gave him my badge."

Marcia, Bruce, and Miriam had been watching from a distance, but when they finally came over to support Amy, they were forced to turn in their credentials, too. At that moment, I trooped into the fair with about twenty other Jews for Jesus. According to a prearranged plan, we were wearing our embroidered denim jackets, "Jesus is a Jew" buttons, and brightly colored *yarmulkahs*. Whenever we are allowed to participate in Jewish activities, we wear clothes that merge with those of everyone else. But when we're excluded or rejected for our beliefs, we usually show up in all our trappings, thus confronting our persecutors in a nonviolent way with what they're doing to us. We stand out in a crowd with those outfits and remind the Jews who reject us of their moral inconsistency and lack of liberalism. They are refusing to let us be Jews and practice our faith freely, and we let them know it. If someone hung up a sign saying, "Everybody welcome but the Jews for Jesus," that would be an invitation for us to appear in full regalia. We won't stand for it. We won't be swept under the rug and denied our rights as human beings and as Jews.

The rabbi in charge of the fair thought he had settled the issue when he took away the guides' credentials. But when the rest of us showed up in our jackets, the JDL people immediately focused their attention on me and began to catcall. I turned my back on them, and at about that time the San Francisco police arrived. The rabbi and the police said that we should go upstairs and discuss what to do, and I agreed. But first I walked over to our group and told them to break up into twos and threes and wander around the fair. As I had expected, the entire JDL contingent went upstairs for the meeting, and thus they were out of our hair for the rest of the evening. We have a saying that every Jew is a *macher,* or a big shot. The JDL certainly proved the maxim that night—all leaders, no followers.

I met for about two hours with the JDL, the rabbi, and the police, and the discussion ranged over everything imaginable.

"Moishe, just one thing," the rabbi asked. "I want your promise as an honorable man that you won't hand out any literature."

"As an honorable man, I promise I won't hand out any," I said, not telling him that we hadn't even brought any tracts with us.

"The main problem is those jackets," Margaret argued. "That jacket is a leaflet in itself."

"It's the right of people to clothe themselves however they want," one of the police inspectors said.

The rabbi said, "Moishe, I know you can wear what you want, but for the peace of Jerusalem, won't you take off your jacket?"

"No," I replied. "I paid for my ticket—we all did. I can wear what I want, and I want to wear this."

But the rabbi then called me away from the others and pleaded, "I don't care what you wear, but do me a favor and take it off."

At that moment I thanked God that I had read Saul Alinsky closely and that we had prayed and discussed ahead of time what the opposition might try to pull on us. Stuart Dauermann had anticipated that the fair officials might try to get us to take off our jackets, so we all agreed that we should wear Jews-for-Jesus T-shirts underneath. I took the jacket off for the rabbi and said, "What do you think is underneath?" There, in bold, living color, perhaps even brighter than the jacket, was "Jews for Jesus" lettering silk-screened on the shirt.

"So what do you want me to do now, take off my T-shirt?" I asked. "What do you think I have underneath that? Nothing."

"All right, already," he said.

The police and the JDL *machers* were still talking, so I decided to slip away and see the fair. They made out complaints, wrote everything down for the police, and in general didn't bother us again until the end of the evening.

We had anticipated the JDL strategy once again because we suspected they'd try to bother us at least once more before we left. The logical place was outside the fair building where they might be able to throw a few punches and kicks, then run away. I arranged to have a couple of plainclothes policemen accompany us outside, and sure enough, the JDL people were all waiting for us in a line. They didn't notice the two plainclothesmen until one of the burly cops said, "You're blocking the walk, move over."

The JDL was completely thwarted that night. All they could do was call us names: *"Meshumad* (traitor, or apostate)! You do it for money. Jesus' mother was a virgin like your mother was a virgin!" But we had won that evening's little game, and they knew it.

In another encounter we had with the JDL, the key figure was not a JDL infiltrator, but one of our own. This Christian woman infiltrated the San Francisco JDL and supplied us regularly with information about their plans to harass us. I received an urgent call one day from our spy and agreed to meet with her at a secret rendezvous to discuss the latest problem. She said the JDL was planning to attack us in some way at an upcoming demonstration against the detention of Soviet Jewry. Two forms of harassment had been suggested at the JDL planning session. One idea involved snatching any Jews-for-Jesus literature we might be carrying at the protest and scattering it in the street. The other possible method of attack was for one of the JDL members to appear wearing a Jews-for-Jesus jacket and carrying a sign saying, "Jesus is a Lesbian."

When I returned from this rendezvous, I immediately called a staff meeting and informed the other Jews for Jesus of the possible offensives against us. We had not planned on taking any Christian literature or wearing our outfits because the other Jewish demonstrators had accepted us as participants. The only literature we intended to use was literature obtained from a Jewish organization on Soviet Jewry. If the JDL attacked us and scattered the leaflets, they would show that their attack was mindless and that to get at us they were willing to hurt the Jewish cause.

The "Jesus is a Lesbian" sign presented a more serious problem. One person suggested we should protest to the person with the sign, but that seemed likely to result in some kind of violence. Someone else said we should protest to the leaders of the demonstration and then walk off. Because we had been instrumental in organizing and leading these demonstrations in the past, that threat might carry some weight. But the best idea—the one we finally settled on—again came from Stuart Dauermann. We decided to stencil "Christians for Kahane" on the back of some T-shirts and then wear these underneath our jackets. Because we knew there could be newspaper photographers and television cameramen there, we foresaw the visual possibilities the situation presented. If the guy with the obscene sign appeared, we'd take off our jackets and coats and form a circle around him with our Kahane emblems prominently displayed for the cameras. We were counting on the fact that most reporters and many viewers would recognize that Meir Kahane is the leader of the JDL. If there is anything Rabbi Kahane is not for, it is Jesus and Christians. This ploy would at least highlight the JDL's involvement with the sign and would serve to confuse the issue.

We were the first to arrive at the demonstration, which was staged in front of the Soviet consulate in San Francisco. By getting there early, we were able to pick the precise site for the demonstration and set the tone we thought proper. As I've mentioned, we're often asked to lead these demonstrations because it's generally accepted that we're among the best qualified, best disciplined demonstrators in the San Francisco community. We've had more experience than other Jewish groups and are familiar with the applicable laws and regulations. We have an understanding with the other Jewish groups that we won't use these occasions to evangelize, and we always live up to our word. Many Jews for Jesus believe in the freedom of Soviet Jewry just as strongly as any other Jews, and we want to be as effective as possible when we demonstrate to support that cause.

We began to march in a tight oval, carrying our signs and chanting, "Let my people go!" You have to keep moving in a demonstration or risk being arrested by the police for standing around and loitering. Representatives from the other Jewish organizations began arriving within the next half hour, and among them, as we had expected, was a small contingent from the Jewish Defense League. One of them, looking straight at me, muttered, "The pigs are here, too. And there's the slob with them." I didn't react but just kept marching. Some of the Defense League people arrived with a big "JDL" sign and were asked by other Jewish leaders not to use it since we were there to demonstrate for Soviet Jews, not to push private causes. But they refused.

The protest swelled to nearly two hundred demonstrators, and we could see people inside the Russian consulate peeking out of their windows, watching us. Television and newspaper reporters and cameramen were there in full force. According to prearranged plan, I was carrying some literature from another organization which protested restrictions on emigration of Soviet Jews. To my relief, though, the obscene sign never appeared. But my relief was short-lived. Seemingly out of nowhere four or five members of the JDL descended on me and pulled me out of the picket line. One woman—I recognized her as Margaret, the one who had infiltrated us—began kicking at me, and the others, all men, shoved and pushed and tore the literature out of my grasp. As Margaret screamed at me, the others scattered the leaflets, hundreds of them, all over the street. "They're taking my literature!" I shouted, staggering back under their onslaught.

Steve Agetstein, who was acting as our photographer that night, jumped into the fray, too, and tried to put himself between me and my attackers. The violence seemed to escalate for a moment but then subsided with the arrival of the police.

None of this melee was reported on television or in the newspapers. But if the press had picked it up and the reporting had been done accurately, the purpose of the JDL attack on me would have seemed senseless, because I was carrying literature that supported the very cause for which they were demonstrating. When the reporters asked what happened, I just smiled, said nothing, and got back into the line.

We usually conduct postmortem evaluations of all our activities, so I immediately launched into an assessment of our tactics when we arrived back at our headquarters after the demonstration.

"First of all, I don't want anybody coming to my aid in a situation like that," I said. "Steve, you shouldn't have jumped into that fight, even though your purpose was nonviolent. Any response from us, no matter how gentle, provokes further violence. If you even say one word to them, you add fuel to the fire. You should just turn around and walk away."

"But I thought it was okay for us to put ourselves between the attackers and the one being attacked, as long as we don't fight back," Steve protested.

"Sometimes—as when one of our girls is being beaten up by some lunatic—that may be the right thing to do. But either I or one of the group leaders will make that decision."

Steve may have made a mistake that evening, but I've found that I also have to be very careful about my own motives and actions. I'm a social-action strategist by inclination, and sometimes I gloat over outsmarting another individual or an opposing organization. Such an attitude can lead to a primary focus on the tactics, rather than on the ultimate goal, which is the glorification of Christ.

I wouldn't want to leave the impression, however, that all or even most of our contacts with the Jewish community are abrasive or combative. One of the most heartening things is to find out how many rabbis and Jewish community leaders are not nearly as hostile to us as one might suppose. I have been involved in numerous radio and television debates with prominent rabbis. On camera and microphone, they have uniformly maintained official resistance. Once off camera and away from the microphone, however, many ask me sincere questions. I was flattered when one rabbi said, "I wish that I were as dedicated to serving the God of Israel and promoting the Torah as you seem to be in your commitment to Christ."

"I'm not serving anyone else besides the God of Abraham, Isaac, and Jacob," I pointed out. "My zeal is not a natural thing but something I get from God."

"I know, I know," he said. "Maybe if I were young and in a different position, I would be prepared to see things your way."

I've encountered only one with whom I've spoken face-to-face in private who was less than respectful to me. We debated on television in New York City, and he was a professor at a rabbinical seminary. After the program, off camera, I extended a hand to him and he said, "I don't shake hands with *mishimudim*. If what you believe is _____, then what you are is _____."

If, as a boy, I had used the word he used, my mother would have scrubbed my mouth out with soap.

There are many Jewish leaders, however, who have a good working relationship with us. And we often find ourselves supporting causes that other Jewish groups advocate. I've mentioned the Soviet Jewry issue. Another example is the film *Jesus Christ Superstar*, which the American Jewish Committee, through its spokesman, Rabbi Marc H. Tanenbaum, has criticized as contributing to anti-Semitism. As I stated earlier, we saw this film and regarded it to be anti-Christian. We also recognized that it maligned the Jewish people, and so we sent out press releases and demonstrated against the movie during the summer of 1973. We were quoted as saying it was "anti-Semitic, anti-Christian, and racist." One leaflet we distributed declared, *"Jesus Christ Superstar* perpetuates the anti-Semitic canard that Jews are 'Christ killers.' The Bible teaches that Jesus *voluntarily* died on the cross to bear the sins of man. The film makes the Jewish leaders, priests, and Pharisees seem to be the 'bad guys' through false stereotypes." This was one of many times that we stood up to the world as Christians and as Jews, showing that the two do not have to be mutually exclusive.

Whether we're in agreement with our Jewish brethren or not, confrontation tactics will probably continue to be necessary, as long as the issue of Jesus continues to be suppressed and ignored. I think our nonviolent approach to confrontation, if kept in proper perspective, is consistent with the way Christ operated. A person can't turn the other cheek if he runs away, or fails to put himself in situations where a blow can be struck. Jesus constantly mixed with the Jewish people, argued with them, forced them to think. So did Paul and the other apostles. In a similar vein, we make our presence and position known, even if we know certain Jewish leaders don't want to hear or see us. Any violence that results comes from them, not from us. The essence of our Christian confrontation tactics is to expose the moral issue and then be ready to accept reproach or even injury for Jesus' sake.

12 THE NEW CREATIVITY

One of the things that has always bothered me about the Protestant church is that aesthetically it is rather sterile. Protestants stress evangelism, social action, and individual piety, and that is certainly putting first things first. But there is also a creative dimension to human existence—literature, art, music. All of these are ways of communicating, but Protestants have often been content to express their faith through old, tired artistic forms, rather than to seek new channels of creative expression.

Jewish culture, far from being stark or sterile, is profoundly sense-oriented. God originally told the Jews not to make any images, apparently because He feared their tendency to worship their own handiwork as idols. But writing and music have always been encouraged among the Jews. The beauty of the Psalms, the logic of the Talmud, and the pulsating rhythms of the *hora* attest to our achievements in those fields. More recently, outstanding Jewish painters, such as Marc Chagall, have flourished.

The Jews for Jesus showed they are the heirs of this rich aesthetic tradition during a *Pesach Seder,* or Passover feast, we had in April, 1973. We wrote our own *Haggadah,* or historical narrative, of how the Jews escaped from the Egyptian Pharaoh in the Book of Exodus. We laced the story with our own songs and ended with a round of traditional Jewish dances. Barry Ellegant, one of our best singers, started the evening by singing the *Kiddush,* or initial blessing over the meal. Then we ate our way through a variety of traditional courses. There was the horseradish, to signify the bitterness and sorrow the Jews suffered as slaves in Egypt. A cup of salt water reminded us of the tears our ancestors shed during their bondage. The rather tasty *charoseth,* a paste made of apples and nuts, brought to mind the bricks the Jews had to make for the Pharaoh's pyramids. The culinary highlight of the evening was the Passover lamb, succulently flavored with garlic.

Appropriately enough, when we had finished with the various prayers and songs, someone requested that the group sing a folk song entitled "Passover Lamb," which was composed by our own Sam Nadler. With Steffi Geiser and Miriam Nadler on acoustical guitars and Stuart Dauermann at the piano, we belted out the words:

Passover Lamb's blood upon the door,
Forming a cross to seal us from death's jaw.

> *And by the blood of the Lamb*
> *We are all set free*
> *And we are free, set free,*
> *We are all set free.*

Pharaoh had the Jews enslaved
Deep within his spell,
But the Lord God intervened
And freed us from that hell.

> *And by the blood of the Lamb . . . .*

God gave us Israel, but we turned away.
God gave us the Law, but we disobeyed.
God gave His only Son to come and set us free.

> *And by the blood of the Lamb . . . .*

But we all did turn away, and we all were lost,
So we took a perfect lamb and nailed Him to the cross.

> *And by the blood of the Lamb . . . .*

Three days He lay, then Jesus did arise
And all who believe will never have to die.

> *And by the blood of the Lamb . . . .*

Sam's song is just one example of how we take a Jewish concept, the Passover, and express the meaning for us as Jews for Jesus. But folk music is not our only means of musical expression. Stuart Dauermann has developed a distinctively Jewish sound, based on Israeli *hora* and Yiddish *freylach* tunes. His compositions make up the bulk of the repertoire of our touring singers, the Liberated Wailing Wall.

Stuart came from what he calls a "culturally Jewish" family and attended a conservative *Talmud Torah,* or Hebrew school, for about four years. He got interested in Jewish music while playing the piano for a jazz band at Jewish resorts in the Catskill Mountains during his summer vacations from college. Except for a couple of isolated marijuana experiences, he was a fairly straight guy, not into the hippie culture like many of our other brothers and sisters. While attending the Manhattan School of Music, Stuart sensed a void in his life, and finally turned to Jesus after reading the New Testament and hearing the witness of several Christian acquaintances.

Stuart's commitment to Christ had a far-reaching impact on his music. I met him at the Beth Sar Shalom center in Manhattan soon after he had made his Christian commitment. "By that time I had my bachelor's degree in music and was about to start teaching in a local junior high school. Moishe suggested I might try to express my faith by composing songs," Stuart explained. "I began by playing the piano and leading the choir at the Beth Sar Shalom center, and gradually started writing a few pieces. When I played them for Moishe, he was very enthusiastic. And after the Jews-for-Jesus movement got under-way, I saved up enough money to quit my teaching job in New York and devote full time to the group's musical efforts."

Stuart's songs, unlike Sam's, have grown out of the Jewish folk-song tradition. Two of the first songs he wrote were a musical version of Psalm 23 and a piece called *"Yehochua Hamashiach* (Jesus the Messiah) Has Come."

"Both of these songs were written in a minor key, but that's not all that makes them Jewish," he said. "There are characteristic rhythms and chord progressions that I learned both from my musical studies and my practical experience in the Catskills. One distinctive feature of these tunes is what is called modal chord changes. For in-stance, some chords in a minor key become major in modal music. Some Semitic dance music has scales which are part minor and part major.

"Examples of this kind of music are the popular *hora,* 'Hava Nagi-lah,' and also a great deal of synagogue music. I used to go to syna-gogue when I was a kid and heard enough liturgical music to acquaint me with the sound. Those liturgical rhythms are slower, but they're similar to the fast Yiddish and Israeli dance songs."

One technique that Stuart has been perfecting is the writing of music that will fit both English and Hebrew lyrics. Working with Eliezer Urbach, a Jewish Christian who is fluent in Hebrew, he com-posed "Hodu et Adoshem," or "Praise the Lord," a lively *hora* that has everyone in the audience clapping and foot-stamping by the time the Liberated Wailing Wall has completed a performance. The sing-ers can alternate verses between Hebrew and English:

> Praise Him, praise Him, praise the Lord.
> Praise the Lord for He is good.
> Praise Him, praise Him, praise the Lord.
> For His wondrous love!

Hodu, hodu et Adoshem
Hodu L'Adoshem Ki Tov
Hodu Hodu et Adoshem
L'Adoshem Ki Tov.

From ev'ry nation He has brought us.
With Messiah's blood He bought us.
By His Spirit He hath taught us.
Let us praise His name!

Min kol hoamim hotzianu,
Uv'dom Hamashiach hoshianu,
V'Limdanu b'rucho
Hallelujah!

"After I became a Jew who believes in Jesus, I found I was more productive than before," Stuart said. "I often write songs when I'm in a joyful mood, and the compositions usually develop rather quickly. I go to the Bible for many of my lyrics, and then the music flows into the words. But there's a problem—I tend to be a rather impetuous person. If a piece takes a lot of time, I may drop it and move on to something else. But in spite of this deficiency, I know the Lord is helping me to be productive. There are many musicians around who are superior to me. They're all over the place. But God is opening up lines of musical communication that I could never have found by myself."

I'm convinced that Stuart's type of music can have a unique place in the Christian church. The roots of Jewish music can often be traced back to biblical traditions and themes, and so the music of the Jews for Jesus has the potential to bring back to the church some of the original Jewish heritage. The Jews for Jesus music tends to make objective statements about God and Christ rather than to express personal sentiments.

"Western church music as we know it today goes all the way back to the Gregorian chants, which in their earliest form strike me as sounding somewhat Semitic," Stuart said. "But the centuries passed and sacred music lost the Semitic flavor, as each Christian era contributed its own distinctive sound. Martin Luther borrowed popular drinking songs to produce hymns like 'A Mighty Fortress Is Our God.' Scottish and English ballads inspired many of our popular country-western gospel songs like 'Amazing Grace.' Negro gospel music has brought in a distinctive style, including antiphonal choral responses as in 'Let My People Go.'

"But the Reformation music was grafted onto the medieval tradition, and the American religious folk music has its roots in secular or nonbiblical traditions. The Jewish rhythms, on the other hand, reflect a Hebrew culture that was the soil from which Christianity sprang. It isn't a question of taking religious words and fitting them to a drinking song. This is a music which expresses the Jewish spirit, the Jewish pathos, the Jewish joy mingled with sorrow, the Jewish exuberance. It's music devoted to God from its very roots, rather than tunes which have Christianity jammed into them."

Our singing group, the Liberated Wailing Wall, is introducing this music to thousands of Christians in church presentations around the country, under the direction of Miriam Nadler. Miriam, an expert on Israeli culture who spent a year studying in Israel, has insisted that the group use instruments that evoke a Middle-Eastern sound. Barry Ellegant plays the recorder, a flutelike wind instrument which produces sounds reminiscent of *Fiddler on the Roof*. Sam Nadler beats rhythms on a drum called a *dunbek,* and the girls in the group—Steffi Geiser, Naomi Green, and Miriam—alternate between the tambourine and acoustical guitars. Stuart rounds out the instruments with his piano, which Miriam says is their substitute for the Middle-Eastern accordion.

But music is only one way we express our creative impulses. Our literature is perhaps an even more important vehicle for communicating our faith to others. Jews often seem to think most effectively in short sayings, or aphorisms. I suppose the Book of Proverbs is proof of this inclination. I myself will frequently jot down a few thoughts when I'm trying to solve a difficult personal problem. Just seeing the words on paper, playing with them, refining them, helps me to think more clearly and arrive at a solution.

One evening after a social gathering, for example, one of the fellows in the group complained to me that one of our girls had worn a skirt that was too short. Most of the young women wear long dresses when they are at a Jews-for-Jesus gathering so that the guys, many of whom come from rather raunchy, sexually-promiscuous backgrounds, won't be tempted to revert to their old ways.

"You know I've got a lust problem, Moishe," the young man said. "I'm trying to develop some self-control and discipline, and it doesn't help to have a girl come into our group and parade around like that."

I thought about his complaint that night and then prayed the next morning, which is the best time of the day for me to wrestle with such problems. I asked God to give this brother the discernment to realize that the girl's actions meant nothing to him. Girls sometimes just want to be seen; but even if he had made a pass at her, it would not have meant she would have been available. This is important for a man in his position to know.

As I prayed and thought, I wrote down a series of aphorisms:

"A girl who makes herself a sex object is unkind to the men about her."

That was clear enough, but it didn't say all I wanted to say. I tried another:

"A man should marry a girl who would make him proud if she were his sister."

That was better. It put the troubled brother's problems in perspective *vis à vis* the girl. I continued to work with the idea:

"A woman who dresses to show too much of her body doesn't have enough of a soul to be attractive to others."

These were all truisms, and there were many exceptions. But this is the way I think of things. It's a rabbinical approach, pondering, thinking a problem through from every angle. My final aphorism went like this:

"Shallow girls wear skimpy clothes."

My wife, Ceil, has collected several hundred of my aphorisms and now they are published in a book called *The Sayings of Chairman Moishe.*

We have combined our penchant for pithy sayings with a knack for satire and irony in our broadside tracts. I've already described some of the broadsides we use at our North Beach demonstrations, but those are only a small segment of the topics we write about. Our tracts are invitations to talk about almost any subject under the sun—hitchhiking, politics, Christian and Jewish holidays, law and order, organic foods, reincarnation, you name it. The tracts are statements about life and about Jesus. They aren't as evangelistic as some people would like, but we find they get the point across and often pique the interest or anger of pedestrians enough to prompt them to write us letters. We write most of the tracts by committee. Several people get together, come up with an idea, and then jointly work up a draft. Steffi and Shelley illustrate them, and we massage the text and art work until we settle on a final product.

The furor over the book by Dr. David Reuben, *Everything You Always Wanted to Know About Sex & Were Afraid to Ask,* inspired a broadside by Steffi Geiser that we entitled: *Everything You Always Wanted to Know About Jesus But Were Afraid to Ask Your Rabbi.*

Though the title may seem flippant, the text involves a rather serious series of questions and answers, such as:

Q: Isn't Jesus *really* only for the Gentiles?

A: Nope. The Messiah was promised to the Jews and came *as* a Jew *through* a Jewish woman, to the Jewish people. And when the Jews did not accept Him (which came as no news to anyone who had read Isaiah 6), He offered salvation to the Gentiles. But that same offer is still good to any Jew who is interested!

One technique we use in writing broadsides is to employ irony by taking a Jewish concept or slogan and "reinterpreting" it in a Christian context. For example, there's a new Jewish youth group called *Hineni,* a Hebrew word meaning, "Here I am." The purpose of this group, one leader has explained, is to get more Jewish young people enthusiastic about Judaism and Jewish culture. In one broadside, Tuvya Zaretsky focused on the word *Hineni* but gave his own version of the true meaning of the word.

The tract depicts a Jewish fellow nuzzling up to an invisible face and asking, "What's a nice four-letter word you can say to God's face?" We give the answer to the question by writing the four-letter Hebrew word which translates into English as *Hineni.* The bulk of the text gives an updated version of the experiences of the Hebrew prophet, Isaiah:

When he beheld the Almighty, our prophet Isaiah trembled and said [here we insert a Hebrew sentence, which we translate loosely], "Oy, am *I* in trouble!" Isaiah knew how he measured up to God. That's why he wrote, "For our transgressions are multiplied before thee, and our sins testify against us" (Isaiah 59:12).

So when God needed a prophet to speak to our people Israel, Isaiah piped up with that four-letter word: "Here Am I."

Now this same Isaiah had once been a confessed *Garbage Mouth,* or as the Bible put it, ". . . a man of unclean lips" (Isaiah 6:15). [One cartoon character at this point asks, "Does he *eat* with that mouth?" and another answers, "Only his enemies should hear from a tongue like that!"]

But God cleansed him and declared: Thine iniquity is taken away, and thy sin purged (Isaiah 6:7). Now Isaiah didn't win any popularity contests with what he had to say . . . . But it was God's message (and *not* Isaiah's bad mouth) that made our people *upset.*

The message God has given us to speak may not be popular either, but it's *true:*

JESUS IS THE MESSIAH OF ISRAEL.

"The Redeemer" that Isaiah wrote of *has* come . . . and is coming *again!*

Join us Jews for Jesus in crying HINENI!

The Jewish Defense League was the target in another broadside drafted by Susan Perlman. The tract is entitled: *J.D.L. Headquarters.* It shows a young man reading a book entitled, *Never Again,* which is the Jewish Defense League's slogan and refers to the Nazi holocaust. In our tract, however, JDL stands for "Jesus Delivers Life," and the slogan is given a different meaning: "NEVER AGAIN shall man be a slave to sin if he asks the Messiah into his heart." The Jewish Defense League apparently thought this broadside was rather effective because they brought a lawsuit to have a Marin County court order us not to distribute any more of the tracts.

The Jewish Defense League sent out news releases to all of the newspapers to announce that they were suing us for infringement on their common-law trademark, which is a clenched fist in a Jewish star. When we went before the judge, we pointed out that our illustration was not of a clenched fist, but rather of an extended index finger giving the "one way" sign of the Jesus Movement. The judge found that we could not use the clenched fist symbol in a Jewish star, the initials JDL, or the slogan, "Never Again," unless we clearly identified the pamphlet as coming from Jews for Jesus. But, as the attorney for the opposition pointed out, under the judge's ruling we could continue to hand out the broadside titled, *JDL Headquarters,* since it met the legal requirements. It had cost us $500 in attorney's fees to defend ourselves, but all of the Jewish newspapers carried the court story and quoted a substantial amount from our tract. There would have been no other way to get so much publicity on such a small amount of money.

I've picked only two of our creative areas, music and tract writing, but there are many others which should bear fruit in the near future. Shelley Korotkin is a very talented painter. She studied at the Academy of Fine Arts in Philadelphia and traveled for awhile in Europe before she came to know Jesus. We expect to have a showing of some of her best works soon.

Mark Winter has done graduate work in film making, and his ultimate ambition is to do some documentaries on our activities. Jh'an Moskowitz, who has a long-standing interest in drama, has organized some of the street-theater presentations.

The difference between Christian artists and those who do not have an abiding religious faith is that our primary aim is to communicate to others what God has done in our lives. The worst sin in our creative expressions is to be boring, and the greatest virtue is to make Jesus attractive for others. My own creative abilities are modest, if not subnormal. But I know the potential of those around me, and I believe we have rediscovered a distinctively Jewish way to present Jesus which has been lying dormant for centuries. There was a large and vital Jewish-Christian group in New Testament times; but their rich and distinctive way of expressing their faith was eventually swallowed by the tidal wave of Gentiles that came into the church. We are now issuing a general invitation to our gentile brethren to return with us to those lost cultural treasures and enjoy, enjoy.

13 PRAYER POWER
AND HOLY GHOST STORIES

God has consistently revealed Himself, from Old Testament times to the present, as a God who acts in history, who intervenes in concrete ways in the lives of men. To many people, the idea of an action-oriented, personal God may seem a superstitious concept of bygone days, not at all suitable for the sophisticated space age. Satan falls into the same category: He just doesn't belong in our civilized contemporary society.

But we Jews for Jesus *know,* beyond any doubt, that the God of the Old and New Testaments is still operating today. We have experienced His power through direct answers to prayer. We also know that the enemy, Satan, is having a field day because people refuse to believe in him and therefore fail to prepare for his attacks.

I've found that God requires two things of me before His power becomes available. First of all, I have to ask. He knows what I want and need even before I ask, but it is up to me to establish a vital spiritual link with concrete requests. Secondly, as the Apostle James indicates in the first chapter of his Epistle, I must ask in faith. Jesus said if our faith is '. . . as a grain of mustard seed" (Matthew 17:20), then we can move a mountain with it. But the faith, the trust, the absolute reliance on God has to be there.

When we get together as a group to pray, I'll often ask the one who feels he has the most faith to offer our supplications to the Lord, and it works! Take a situation about which Susan Perlman and I were concerned. One of the primary goals we have here in California is that each person be mobile, be able to meet a troubled person several miles away or move out to a demonstration at a moment's notice. Such mobility requires automobiles, and most of our young people can't afford one, especially when they first arrive here. Susan was in that predicament.

"I had never driven before I came to California, and I took the driver's test over and over again but kept failing it," she said. "As I was trying to pass, Moishe and I prayed together that the Lord would in some unique way give us five hundred dollars for a used car that I could drive. On my fifth try, I passed the test. Almost simulta-

neously, we got a call from a lady in Los Angeles who was interested in our work. Without any prodding on our part, she offered to
donate her car. It was a 1965 Chevrolet, which at the time was valued
at almost exactly five hundred dollars."

But God wasn't finished with that car yet. We found that it needed
some work—a valve job and repairs on a defective camshaft which a
mechanic estimated would cost $328. Money is very short with us,
but we've learned to rely on the Lord. Susan and I prayed again. Then
I remembered something: I asked her if she had filed her income-tax
return, and she said no. After she filed, she got a refund which came
to $322. I'm sure that God put the idea into my head, just as He
provided us with the car in the first place. We've gotten used to praying for specific amounts and specific things, and as long as we're
working and doing our share, we have found God is faithful in provid-
ing for us.

Mark Winter had a similar experience after he joined our fellowship. "I hadn't been home for a visit since becoming a Christian, and
I felt strongly that God wanted me to see my family," he said. "The
problem was that I didn't have enough money for the round trip to
New York, so I began to pray about it one evening during the summer of 1972. I didn't tell anyone else what I was praying for because
I didn't want to be influenced in any way. I just wanted this to be a
matter between me and God.

"I called my family the next evening to talk to them for a couple
of minutes, but the person who answered the phone was a girl who
had become a Christian in California and had returned a few months
before to her home in New Jersey. Frankly, I didn't want to talk to
her. I felt she was preventing me from talking with my sister, and so
I sort of put her off, you know, was rather short with her. It was a
horrible thing, but that was just the way I reacted.

"Well, she told me she had to say something before she got off the
phone, and I reluctantly agreed, thinking all the time about the phone
bill I was running up. She said that when she got up that morning,
she knew there was something she had to do. She sensed that God
wanted her to buy me a plane ticket home, and so she had gone to a
travel agent and bought one. 'I just mailed it to you this morning,' she
said, 'It's between you and the Lord, what you want to do with it.'
Then she got off the phone without giving me a chance to reply. I
was stunned. God had given me a concrete answer to my prayer only
a day after I had asked. That's one of the heaviest things that's ever
happened to me."

Sometimes I also wonder if God doesn't employ an accounting staff. Stuart Dauermann is a full-time volunteer like most of the other Jews for Jesus, so he has to live off what he's saved. He brought a piano out here from New York, but it recently went out of tune, and he didn't have the money to fix it. I had received a fifty-dollar check in the mail, and I asked God whether I should give it to Stuart for his general living expenses, or use it to tune the piano, or do something else with the money. Because all of us enjoy Stuart's music, I finally decided to ask for contributions for the piano tuning at one of our Bible-study meetings. Having announced it would cost about thirty dollars for the tuning, I passed a hat around to the forty or so people there. The hat came back with eighty-one dollars in donations. That was a direct answer to all the financial worrying I'd been doing: Stuart would get fifty dollars for his living expenses, thirty dollars would go for the piano, and the fifty-dollar check could be used for another purpose. Such precise responses of God are a commonplace occurrence for us.

But our prayers are by no means directed only to our own physical needs. For example, Miriam Nadler got a call from her mother that one of her nephews had developed a malignant tumor at the base of his brain. After he had been admitted to a Maryland hospital and underwent surgery, the doctors found they couldn't remove the growth because of its dangerous location. We all began to pray regularly for the boy's condition and other Christian groups on the East Coast also asked God's help.

"My nephew stayed in intensive care for about a week after the operation, hovering between life and death," Miriam said. "He was then transferred to another hospital for cobalt treatments. Before the treatments began, they decided to take some final X rays, but this time they found only traces of a tumor. Another operation confirmed that there were only traces, but no mass. He now has a tube inserted into his brain to drain off excess fluids, but he's improved dramatically. He's already returned to his school classes, and the only restriction on him is that he can't engage in heavy physical activity. The whole experience really blew my mind. There's no question that God answered our prayers."

In addition to these concrete answers to prayer, some Jews for Jesus have found that God communicates through dreams and visions. Barry Ellegant, for example, became confused and uncertain just after he became a Christian. "I wasn't sure where I was going," Barry explained. "But then God spoke to me in an incredible way. I had a

vision one day—I saw the heavenly Jerusalem. I saw the saints lined
up as an impregnable army. There was no way they could be defeated.
It was unbelievable. There was a wall before the city, and the saints,
wearing their battle array and holding shields and spears, were lined
up in front of the wall. They were standing motionless, looking in one
direction, as though they were waiting for a signal. I think they were
getting ready for the final battle with Satan. It was quite vivid, so
vivid that words can't really describe the scene. I think God was
showing me this overwhelming force to assure me that I wasn't alone,
that the church and the saints are very real and I am part of their
mighty legions. We are all an impregnable army."

Although I believe that God intervenes in our lives with great
regularity, I'm afraid that we also experience some less-than-construc-
tive supernatural intervention from another quarter. Satan, who took
over as prince of this world when Adam abdicated his God-given trust,
is always giving us trouble. He uses the activities at North Beach to
lure the lonely away from constructive answers to their problems. He
helps to erect barriers between the Jews for Jesus and the rest of the
Jewish community. And he succeeds in subtle ways in diverting us
from always following God's directions.

Satan acted in a very personal way against us on one occasion
when he used the daring and flirtatious nature of a Jewish-Christian
woman for his malicious ends. I had gone to sleep at my usual time
one night, but I woke up in the early-morning hours in a cold sweat.
I had dreamed that the woman, whom I'll call Judy, was being pulled
toward a yellowish, abstract figure that was clearly the devil. I was
pulling her from the other direction, but Satan said, "I'll have her.
She's mine, and I'll have her yet."

I sensed that this was no ordinary dream, so I immediately got on
the phone and called Judy's apartment, but she wasn't at home. She
wasn't active with our group on a regular basis, but I knew her well
enough to realize it was unusual for her to be out that late. I became
worried. I waited about ten minutes and called again, but still there
was no answer. Deciding that something might be wrong, I dressed
and drove to her place, but there was no answer when I rang the
bell. I also noticed that her car was gone. I then returned home and
called her place about every half hour until I finally fell asleep on
my sofa.

Later that morning, bleary-eyed from lack of sleep, I went to her
apartment, and she answered the door.

"What happened?" I asked.

"What do you mean?" she replied.

"I know something happened last night," I said and described my dream. She went white and then broke down and began to cry. The story came out in sobs: Contrary to good common sense, she had picked up a young male hitchhiker the previous evening while driving home from a Christian rally in San Francisco. She knew she was doing the wrong thing, but she was confident that she could handle any problem that arose. Unfortunately, she hadn't anticipated that he would draw a knife.

He forced her to pull off onto a deserted side road and held her for several hours, making her perform every imaginable natural and unnatural sex act with him. He then told her to drop him off in a nearby congested urban area, and he disappeared into the morning crowd.

I'm convinced I had a battle with the devil in that dream. I was on one side, trying to convince Judy to be careful and prudent and to remember her allegiance to God. Satan was opposing me, attempting to use her tendency to flirt and disobey. Satan won that skirmish, but in some ways Judy is a stronger Christian for the experience. I feel quite certain he won't achieve an ultimate victory over her.

After Christians have a few vivid experiences with God and the devil, there may be a tendency to become too spooky. Some believers tend to see supernatural interventions when they're not really there, or to embellish or exaggerate actual encounters with the supernatural. They fool themselves into thinking they have seen or heard or experienced something that never occurred. A person who is good at telling these "Holy Ghost stories" may find that he has a power over others, especially those who are younger and less experienced. Also, although we have experienced a great deal of startling supernatural intervention, I am reluctant to emphasize these incidents, because I don't want to lead others to rely on miracles instead of making an effort to trust God and then work hard to solve their problems.

As the leader of the Jews for Jesus, I enjoy a certain respect and authority in the group. The others are ready to disagree with me on any point, but if I tell them God told me something, they are likely to believe me because they know I always try to be honest about my spiritual experiences. Because of the danger of becoming too authoritative for my own good, I constantly warn the others to evaluate each supernatural event carefully in light of what they know to be true from their own experience with God and the Scriptures.

Sometimes I'll find a Christian who will try to manipulate others by using the "language of Zion." The typical line might go like this: "Oooooh, Brother Moishe, the Spirit of God is showing me some things about you. Take those clothes you wear. They're too flashy for your own good, and I think He would like you to change your ways. And you're associating with the wrong kind of people, too many of those hippies. You know you're not where you should be with the Lord. Now the first thing you should do is put all these matters under the blood. Walk in the newness of the life that He's going to give you. And believe me, He's *going* to give it to you. I *know*. You don't realize how much joy and peace and strength you can have if you're ready to yield your heart to Him."

Now some people might laugh at such a performance, but others, less sophisticated, might get spooked and mesmerized by this kind of sales talk. And that's what it is—manipulative sales talk. The guy could as easily walk behind the counter in a clothing store and say, "I've got a pair of shoes for you, Mr. Rosen, and I *know* you're going to love them. Try them on. I think you'll like the price, too. They're the best pair of shoes you've ever had. They'll last you for the rest of your life. Just touch the top of this leather. You'd be ashamed to walk away from a buy like this."

I was a salesman before becoming an evangelist, and so I know that excessive puffing of the product in either field can have an unhealthy impact on unsuspecting, undiscerning individuals. If I tried to manipulate the other Jews for Jesus in this way, the result would be disastrous. The spontaneity, the banter back and forth, would be lost, and their need for an independent relationship with the Lord would remain unfulfilled. God's own activities in this world are sufficiently amazing without my making up supernatural feats to bolster His reputation.

14 JEWS FOR JESUS—
THE FUTURE OF THE MOVEMENT

Biblical Judaism is a messianic faith, and a steadily increasing number of Jews are recognizing this fact and affirming Jesus as their Messiah. Every qualified observer, including rabbis who would like to pretend we don't exist, acknowledges that there are now thousands of young Jews for Jesus and countless older Hebrew Christians spreading the Good News in this country and abroad.

I have been preaching the gospel to my fellow Jews for more than two decades in many sections of the country, but until the late 1960s the number of Jews coming to Christ represented only a trickle. Now, the trickle has turned into a flood, which carries significant implications for the church, for the Jewish community, and perhaps even for the final destiny of the world itself.

1. *The Church*
The Jesus people's movement in general has brought a youthful enthusiasm back into the church. The charismatic movement has helped revive an exuberant New Testament approach to the Holy Spirit. But the Jews for Jesus offer something additional—a return to the Hebrew roots of the Christian experience. Jesus was a Jew. All the early Christian leaders were Jewish. The God of the New Testament is also the God of the Old. But often, gentile Christians ignore their Jewish heritage. They forget that gentile Christians have been grafted into the family of Abraham, according to Paul in Romans 11. To understand the full import of the cultural and spiritual roots of their faith, gentile Christians should delve more deeply into the experiences of God's chosen people. We Jews for Jesus are the bridge that can enable our gentile brethren to join in probing these rich reservoirs of our common heritage.

In more general terms, our experience has taught me the importance of mobilizing Christian young people for God's work. I'm convinced that most young believers would benefit for the rest of their lives from an intensive, action-oriented period of spiritual service. Many young people have stayed several months or even years with us and then have moved on to other sections of the country, carrying with them a profound and creative commitment to communicating the gospel. How might the church establish such a program for young people? One answer would be to set up a Christian peace corps, with a one- or two-year term of service. The Mormons already have a similar program, and I think the traditional Christian churches might do well to think along the same lines.

2. The Jewish Community

Most Jews will continue to be interested in what we're doing, and I predict that greater numbers will turn to Christ. The Jewish establishment, on the other hand, will continue to produce opponents for us.

One particular area of concern for me is that some parents might target us for the kidnapping ventures that have plagued other Christian youth groups. Absurd as it seems to those who know the Jews for Jesus, some people still insist that I'm a master mesmerizer who exercises unnatural powers over younger Christians. I mentioned in another context that most Jews are *machers*, or independent big shots, by nature, and the Jews for Jesus are no exception to this rule. If we seem better disciplined or more capable of following a predetermined plan of action than most of our opponents, it's because of our love for each other and for Christ, not because of some kind of mass hypnotism.

Our experiences with relatives are echoed in the prediction Jesus made: "For I am come to set a man at variance against his father, and the daughter against her mother, and the daughter-in-law against her mother-in-law. And a man's foes shall be they of his own household. He that loveth father or mother more than me is not worthy of me . . ." (Matthew 10:35–37).

Some parents, upset over their child's commitment to Jesus, have become convinced I am paying their sons and daughters money to stay here with me. Others have tried to buy their kids away by offers of further schooling or attractive trips. I myself am constantly asked a typically Jewish question by television interviewers and even the average Jew on the street: "How much are they paying you? You must be getting millions to do the crazy things you do." I always tell them the truth—that I'm getting the salary of a well-paid secretary, or a schoolteacher, and that's it. But that answer is never acceptable, because who would do such eccentric things and make such outlandish claims without getting a significant reward for the effort and inevitable abuse? Unless, of course, I'm crazy. Or unless I'm convinced beyond the shadow of a doubt that it's all true and that my ultimate reward will come from God.

3. *The World*

Many believe that we are living in the end times and that the Second Coming of Christ is imminent. Some people are even using the increasing numbers of Jews who are accepting Christ as an argument that these are the last days. They rely on Romans 11, where the Apostle Paul indicates that just before Jesus returns, the number of Gentiles who accept Christ will fall off, but the Jews will begin turning to Him in unprecedented numbers. I wouldn't be at all surprised to see a great Jewish revival in the near future, because there are definite tendencies in that direction right now.

The Jews-for-Jesus movement started without a name. It represented a spiritual ground swell which swept me along after it was already in progress. Our group in California contributed the slogan *Jews for Jesus* that became the generic term for the thousands of young Jews who were reclaiming their heritage. And we have been instrumental in formulating the tactics and communications techniques that are proving effective in many other places, hundreds and thousands of miles from our California headquarters. At the time of this writing, there are Jews for Jesus in most of the large Jewish population centers of the world, and we receive hundreds of letters asking for samples of our materials and instruction in our methods.

First came the movement, and then came the name, and now it has become necessary to establish a separate organization to continue fostering our unique testimony. The American Board of Missions to the Jews, our previous sponsor in San Francisco, gave $69,000 in 1972, and our project cost half again that in 1973. According to the ink orders from the company that manufactures our duplicating machine, we turned out four million pamphlets in three years. Our Jews-for-Jesus project was getting too big for one sponsor and we felt that our ministry could no longer be restricted to San Francisco. So with regret I had to accept the termination of my working relationship with the American Board of Missions to the Jews.

In forming the new support organization, which is called Hineni Ministries, we had no outside help, just the overriding conviction that God wants us to continue. Although we estimate that the ministry we want to carry out in our first year of organization life will cost $108,000, we are entering this ministry with $4000 we managed to get together. Our financial future, from a worldly point of view, may seem uncertain. But we've learned to trust and believe in God. We know He has something big, something of cosmic proportions in store for us and for other Christians.

I don't like to nail myself down on the issue, to say without reservation that I know Christ will come tomorrow, or next year, or before the year 2000. But I have a strong sense that something is going to happen. I live every day as though I believe Christ is returning soon, because the Bible says to live that way. Even if I can't say with assurance that the Jews-for-Jesus movement represents a definite sign of the last times, I will say this: All the conditions are *go* for the church to be launched into orbit any day with Jesus. In the meantime, while we're watching and waiting, let me say: God bless you . . . and *shalom!*

Moishe Rosen
P.O. Box 309
Corte Madera,
California   94925